100

LEARNING GAMES

3 TO 5

Easy-to-play games

Supporting early learning

Stages of development

LINDA MORT

CREDITS

British Library Cataloguing-in-Publication Data A catalogue record for this book is available from the British Library.

ISBN 0 439 98335 5

Author
Linda Mort

Illustrations
Gaynor Berry

Editor
Lesley Sudlow

Assistant Editor
Saveria Mezzana

Series Designer
Anna Oliwa

Designer
Anna Oliwa

Text © 2002 Linda Mort
© 2002 Scholastic Ltd

Designed using Adobe Pagemaker

Published by Scholastic Ltd,
Villiers House,
Clarendon Avenue,
Leamington Spa,
Warwickshire CV32 5PR

Visit our website at www.scholastic.co.uk
Printed by Belmont Press

1 2 3 4 5 6 7 8 9 0   2 3 4 5 6 7 8 9 0 1

Acknowledgements:

The publishers gratefully acknowledge permission to reproduce the following copyright material:

© **Derek Cooknell:** p16, p17

© **Corbis:** p8

© **Digital Vision Ltd:** Cover, p5, p6

© **Image 100 Ltd:** p37, p38

© **Ingram Publishing:** p3, p4, p5, p7

© **Photodisc, Inc:** p1, p4, p42, p87, p114

© **John Fortunato/SODA:** p10, p18, p20, p23, p24, p34, p53, p54, p56, p62, p67, p72, p74, p77, p81, p82, p85, p97, p112, p124

© **Dan Howell/SODA:** p7, p52, p58, p61, p69, p81, p88, p93, p122

© **Ken Karp/SODA:** p31, p68

© **James Levin/SODA:** p14, p15, p27, p36, p39, p41, p53, p55, p59, p73, p111, p112, p123

© **Dan Powell/SODA:** p9, p115, p120

© **Ross Whitaker/SODA:** p47, p96, p98, p104, p105

© **Photodisc via SODA:** p80

© **Stockbyte:** Cover, p1, p3, p4, p6, p8, p42

Every effort has been made to trace copyright holders and the publishers apologise for any inadvertent omissions.

CONTENTS

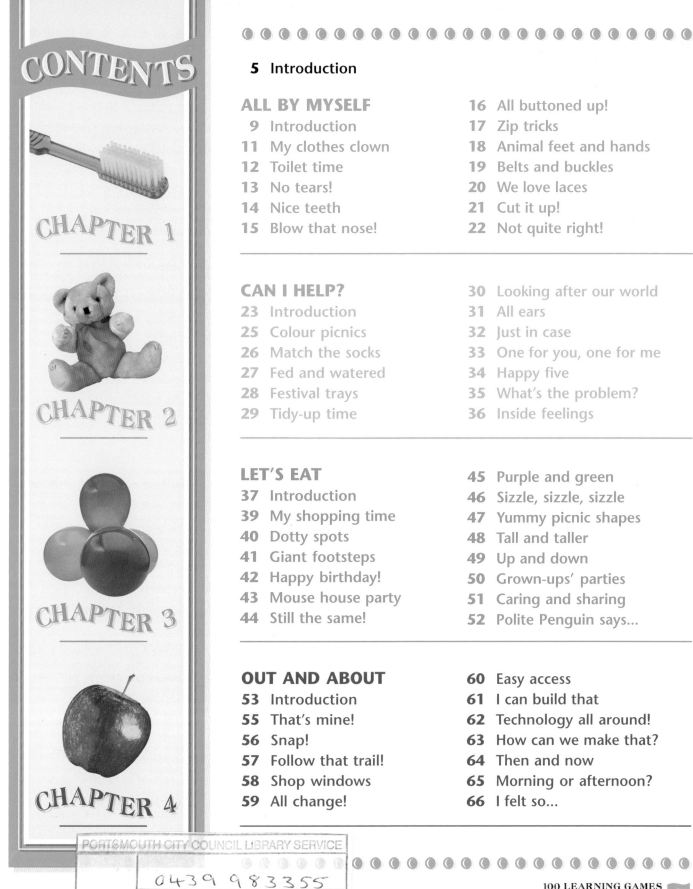

CHAPTER 1

CHAPTER 2

CHAPTER 3

CHAPTER 4

CONTENTS

CHAPTER 5

CHAPTER 6

CHAPTER 7

CHAPTER 8

100 LEARNING GAMES

INTRODUCTION

Learning through play

Emma, aged four and three quarters, has recently been given the video of *Cinderella*. She has become enchanted with the story and is animatedly 'playing Cinderella' with three friends and her baby brother, Ben. She has the starring role and also 'directs' the others.

As the oldest child, Emma takes great pride in showing the others her writing skills. Using a mixture of letter-like shapes and elaborate squiggles, she produces an invitation that, unfortunately, is too big to fit inside any envelope. As she is loath to fold the invitation, the game almost does not get started until Dad, unobtrusively keeping an eye on things as he reads the newspaper, suggests rolling it into a 'scroll from the olden days'. They find a tassel from an unused gift of a calendar to tie around it.

Emma successfully deals with the problem of there being only one sparkly dress by prudently allowing the 'fairy godmother' to wear the only tiara. She is pleased with her idea of using an orange football as a pumpkin and, when one of her friends points out that it is too small, she replies, 'Well, it's only a *baby* pumpkin!'. Emma comes up with the idea of using Ben's toddle truck as a 'coach' and skilfully propels herself along to the 'ball'. Throughout, she provides a lively running commentary – 'And then we all dance around and then the clock strikes twelve o'clock midnight, doiing, doiing, doiing!' – which keeps the other children interested.

Parental role

At this point, Ben, who was given the role of a horse by Emma, wants to join in the dancing, too, although rather over-enthusiastically. Emma complains to Dad that Ben 'keeps spoiling the game', so Dad decides to scoop him up and tactfully remove him from the scene because he needs some 'oats and hay.'

The role of Emma's father, on hand to support and develop the play unnoticed, is very important in enabling her game to be an enjoyable and successful

learning experience. The most valuable kind of play arises from children's self-chosen, spontaneous ideas, supported and sensitively developed and extended by adults. These kinds of play experiences will help children to make progress in their learning. Between the ages of three and five, they find out about the world through active learning and exploring through the senses in all kinds of play – physical, creative, cognitive and social.

Child development stages

Between the ages of three and four, children can be said to literally 'find their feet' in the world, in the way that they delight in their rapidly developing skills of running, jumping, climbing and tricycle-pedalling. They learn how to throw and kick a ball, and begin to take pleasure in drawing, writing in their own way and cutting. They tell themselves long stories in the present tense, projecting their experiences on to their playthings and 'talking through' their happy or troubling experiences in role-play or imaginative play. Children are hungry for knowledge and new vocabulary to be able to put into words what they discover through their physical actions, looking, listening, touching, tasting and smelling, learning to use such words as 'upside-down', 'speckled', 'jingling', 'prickly' and 'sour'. They constantly ask questions beginning with 'what', 'where', 'why' and 'how' and begin to be aware of the significance of the words and numbers that they see all around them. Socially, they develop from playing alongside others to enjoying their companionship, which includes learning about sharing and turn-taking.

Between the ages of four and five, children develop into energetic, confident, agile and, sometimes, daring 'movers'. They begin to enjoy group throwing and catching games, they can kick a ball into a 'goal' and start to devise their own 'rules', based on notions of 'fair play'. They will persevere in practising new skills such as using a bat and ball. At this age, they start to add detail to their pictures, colour them, form letters and numbers correctly, begin to read and solve real mathematical problems, for example, 'I need two more, please'. They now use the past and future tense, and can plan and reflect on their actions. They begin to think in the abstract, using language as a tool for thinking, as they start to use words to represent their experiences, thoughts, explanations and feelings. They empathise with others and can represent this in group dramatic play, for example, 'I'm crying because my bossy sisters are horrible to me and won't let me go to the ball!'.

INTRODUCTION

Child guidance

Throughout this time of rapid development, it is better if you are guided by your child in terms of what he is interested in, and what he wants and needs to learn. Through observation and unhurried chats, you can ensure that your input is not 'out of context' and is 'in tune' with your child's wavelength. It can sometimes be tempting to interfere in, and take over, your child's experiences. When in doubt, 'tread softly' and think of your child as an 'explorer' with yourself as the 'expert travel guide' who presents opportunities to extend horizons safely, but leaves the explorer to make his own discoveries.

Games

All the games in this book are designed to help you to support, develop and extend your child's play experiences, and help him to learn through games based on his initial interests and enthusiasms. Carefully watch your child playing and talk to him about what he knows, thinks and feels, as well as what he finds fun and fascinating, whether at home, at the childminder's or at an early years setting.

The games featured are enjoyable and will appeal to your child's sense of novelty, fun and 'hands-on' learning. They are designed to stimulate lots of ongoing conversation and learning through 'talking and doing', and require the absolute minimum of preparation using everyday items. The instructions are suitable for one or two children at home or at a childminder's, and are very easy to adapt for larger groups in a playgroup, crèche, nursery or Reception class.

Daily routines and experiences

Each chapter is related to an everyday routine and experience of young children in their daily lives, starting with early morning getting up, washing and dressing in 'All by myself' (Chapter 1). Games based on helping and getting along with others are provided in 'Can I help?' (Chapter 2). 'Let's eat' (Chapter 3) details games based on healthy snack times and can also help to develop everyday mathematical understanding. The games in 'Out and about' (Chapter 4) promote children's scientific awareness, while creative pretending games are featured in 'Let's pretend' (Chapter 5). 'Quiet times' (Chapter 6) gently helps to develop early reading, writing, listening and speaking skills. 'Lively times' (Chapter 7) offers lively games to promote active and physical development, and there are quiet and relaxing games to play in 'Winding down' (Chapter 8).

Foundation Stage

In order for parents, carers and early years practitioners to share a common language, and to agree aims when talking about the progress that their children are making in all the Areas of Learning, the Qualifications and Curriculum Authority (QCA) published the *Curriculum Guidance for the Foundation Stage* (2000). The aim of this document is to guide parents and early years settings in providing activities and experiences to help children to make progress in their development and learning.

All early years settings that receive grant funding for the education of three- to five-year-olds are required to plan and provide an appropriate curriculum. Although children's learning cannot be compartmentalised, the document divides learning in the early years into six Areas of Learning for ease of planning and for purposes of tracking progress. They are:

- Personal, social and emotional development
- Communication, language and literacy
- Mathematical development
- Knowledge and understanding of the world
- Physical development
- Creative development.

In each Area of Learning, there are Early Learning Goals that describe the levels expected to be achieved by the end of the Foundation Stage, and there are Stepping Stones relating to knowledge and skills that adults can help children to acquire in order to progress towards the Early Learning Goals.

Each chapter in this book begins with an introduction that highlights some of the main child development stages relevant to the chapter. Your child should not be expected to pass through all the stages in the order presented – some concepts will appear to be understood quite quickly, while others will take much longer. Each game begins with a 'Learning opportunity' that gives a general description of what your child can learn. 'You will need' provides a list of the resources needed to play the game. The Stepping Stones and Early Learning Goals relevant to the game are also featured. 'Sharing the game' gives instructions on how to play. Finally, 'Taking it further' suggests one or two further ideas to extend the game, if appropriate for your child.

The ideas suggested in this book can be applied equally well to the documents on pre-school education published for Scotland, Wales and Northern Ireland.

CHAPTER 1

Provided that children are loved, nurtured and protected, they all have an innate drive to be able to look after themselves. They want to be able to organise their world, be clean, dress themselves and eat with others, sharing the rules and conventions of the people closest to them, as long as these rules make sense to them and appeal to them at all levels. If we try to follow our children's lead, watch carefully as they play and listen to them, we can be helped enormously in working out how to help them along the road to independence in the areas of hygiene, dressing and eating.

ALL BY MYSELF

CLEAN AND HEALTHY

By the age of three, most children have accomplished the main skills involved in washing their hands and face and going to the toilet, although certainly not all children will be toilet-trained. Those who are trained may still have the occasional 'accident' and will need imaginative reminders from time to time about how to manage their clothing, for example, when going to the toilet so that 'splashing' can be avoided. By the age of four to four and a half, children can start to be expected to use tissues or a handkerchief by themselves. Although children of three can manage to brush their

teeth to a certain extent, dentists recommend that an adult should continue to brush a child's teeth, standing behind the child, until the age of about nine. Given children's love of independence, a compromise solution could be 'my turn, now your turn'. From the age of six, children may use an electric toothbrush, under supervision.

How you can help

● If your child appears reluctant or resistant in any area of personal hygiene, try to encourage her to tell you what is worrying her.
● Watch and talk to your child when she uses the toilet. Chat with other carers about any problems that you may be able to foresee. Clinging tights or dungarees with 'fiddly' clasps might be causing difficulties at playgroup, or maybe the use of a kind of toilet paper that is different from the one at home is making her anxious.

• Above all, an adult's willingness to get involved, with a sense of humour and imagination, will often save the day. This is especially true in the area of role-play. If your child is very anxious about an experience, for example, hair-washing, it can be very beneficial to play 'Hairdressers' with her (see the activity 'No tears!' on page 13).

• Sometimes your child may just need a simple, new idea, such as a jolly rhyme (see, for example, the rhyme 'I Can' on page 125) to rekindle her interest in what can come to seem like a 'chore'.

DRESSING

By the age of three, most children will have mastered putting on simple clothes such as hats, trousers and skirts, and by the age of four, most children can manage underwear, socks, jumpers and so on. Between the ages of four and five, many children can start to practise

managing tights, buckles, buttons and zips. Nearly all children of this age have the incentive of starting school and knowing that these skills are highly prized at 'big school'. Most children of five can start learning to tie shoelaces.

How you can help

• If at all possible, try to resist the temptation to continue dressing your child yourself because it is quicker!

• It is often useful to help your child to develop dressing skills by kneeling or sitting directly behind her, and gently guiding her hands, as you talk her through the process.

• Join in with fun role-play with your child and become, for example, the 'mixed-up coat shop assistant' who puts coats on her customers back to front!

• Help your child to help herself by organising her clothes storage, so that she can have some say in choosing what to wear. For example, display large picture labels on drawers and wardrobes (see the activity 'My clothes clown' on page 11).

EATING

By the age of three, most children can manage to eat with a fork and spoon and pour from a jug. By the age of four, many children will have developed the skill of using a knife for spreading, and from the age of four, they can start to use a knife and fork.

How you can help

• Although it can be difficult for members of a family to sit down together at meal times, try whenever possible to arrange for at least one adult, such as yourself, to eat something with your child.

• Sit next to your child so that she can see how you hold your cutlery. However, do not be in a hurry to rush these skills.

• By sharing meals enjoyably and playing 'House' and 'Cafés' with you, your child will progressively develop these skills.

In this chapter you will find ideas focusing mainly on developing the self-care skills that any child needs, for example, after waking up in the morning and getting herself ready for her day. Most of these skills form part of the Personal, social and emotional development component of the early years Foundation Stage. Of course, children's learning is not compartmentalised, so when your child looks into her tissue and tries to 'count the germs', she is adding to her developing understanding of the science of keeping healthy.

LEARNING OPPORTUNITY
● To get clothes ready for the next day.

YOU WILL NEED
A child's plastic, triangular clothes hanger; two dolly pegs; card; scissors; sticky tape; glue; felt-tipped pens; wool; glitter (optional).

STEPPING STONE Take initiatives and manage developmentally appropriate tasks.

EARLY LEARNING GOAL
Personal, social and emotional development: Select and use activities and resources independently.

My clothes clown

Sharing the game
● Tell your child that it is very grown-up to organise our clothes at bedtime ready for the next day, so that we do not have to rush around looking for things in the morning.

● Suggest to your child that you make a 'Clarence Clown' or 'Clarabella Clown' together to help to organise her clothes every night for the next morning.

● Cut out a card oval, approximately 20cm long, and let your child draw a clown's face on it. Add glitter if desired.

● Help your child to glue on wool for the hair.

● Attach the clown's face to the clothes hanger with sticky tape.

● Decide with your child what she is going to wear the next day, then help her to find the items and put them on the clothes hanger. Fold vests and pants over the bottom of the hanger, and clip on trousers or skirts with the pegs. Socks and tights can be put inside shoes and positioned underneath the clown.

● Help your child to hang 'Clarence' or 'Clarabella' on to her bedroom door or wardrobe handle, or on to a hook (at her height).

● Encourage your child to also put her school bag and PE bag (if applicable) next to 'Clarence' or 'Clarabella'.

Taking it further
● Occasionally, suggest that your child might like to choose a special clothes theme, for example, clothes all of one colour, pattern or texture (shiny, glittery and so on).

LEARNING OPPORTUNITIES
● To manage to pull clothes up and down.
● To remember to flush the toilet and to wash hands.

YOU WILL NEED
A doll or teddy bear with 'loose' trousers; pair of children's jogging bottoms and loose-fitting pants.

 THINK FIRST!
Be aware of other cultures in which toilet paper may not be used.

 STEPPING STONE
Shows awareness of own needs with regard to eating, sleeping and hygiene.

 EARLY LEARNING GOAL
Physical development: Recognise the importance of keeping healthy and those things which contribute to this.

Toilet time

Sharing the game
● Use a doll or teddy bear to demonstrate to your child how he should push his trousers right down to his ankles when he goes to the toilet.
● In the early months after toilet training, dress your child in loose jogging bottoms and loose-fitting pants.
● Each morning, mime with your child the actions of pushing down his jogging bottoms and pants to his ankles and pulling them up again, so that he is aware that he can do it.
● Tell your child (not too alarmingly!) about invisible germs and how he must always flush the toilet and wash his hands straight away after using the toilet, so that he does not get a tummy ache.

● Teach this rhyme to your child:
Flush! Flush! Flush!
Toilet germs all gone!
Wash! Wash! Wash!
Hand germs all gone!

Taking it further
● Tell your child that a good way to wipe himself and to keep himself clean is to make a special 'glove' over his fingers.
● Demonstrate to your child how to pull approximately four sections of paper from a roll, fold the paper in half and hold it over his fingers, securing it with his thumb.
● If your child's nursery or school uses 'flat pack' interleaved toilet paper, buy one pack (available from supermarkets) and let your child become familiar with using this.

LEARNING OPPORTUNITY
● To learn how to wash at the wash basin.

YOU WILL NEED
A wash basin.

STEPPING STONE
Demonstrate a sense of pride in own achievement.

EARLY LEARNING GOAL
Personal, social and emotional development: Dress and undress independently and manage their own personal hygiene.

No tears!

Sharing the game

● Your child is probably very proud of being able to wash her hands, but sometimes the novelty wears off! Getting soap in her eyes may make her avoid face-washing. If so, sing this song together at the wash basin to the tune of 'The Grand Old Duke of York' (Traditional):

When we wash our hands,
We twirl the soap around
And keep our eyes wide op-e-en
When we wash our hands!

But when we wash our faces
We close our eyes tight shut
When we wash our fa-ay-aces
We close our eyes tight shut!

Then we rinse the soap off
Then we rinse the soap off
And rub-a-dub with a towel
Until we're nice and dry!

● For an older child who can wash her neck and ears, sing this alternative second verse:

But with our faces, necks and ears
Our faces, necks and ears
We close our eyes tight shut
And don't get any tears!

Taking it further

● Play 'Hairdressers' with your child. Invite her to be the hairdresser and encourage her to put a towel around you, comb water and a little baby shampoo into your hair, put a shower cap on you and massage your head through the cap, then rinse your hair at the 'backwash' (possibly using a shower attachment). Then reverse the roles by letting your child wear goggles, with a flannel over her forehead if necessary. Improvise a 'backwash' by placing a high chair (leaving out the tray), if possible, in front of the wash basin or at the side of the bath.

LEARNING OPPORTUNITY
● To practise brushing teeth.

YOU WILL NEED
A box of small, white tooth-shaped mints, such as Tic-tacs, or 20 small pieces of white card; Blu-Tack; small plastic plate; child's toothbrush; small stand-up mirror.

STEPPING STONE
Show some understanding that good practices with regard to exercise, eating, sleeping and hygiene can contribute to good health.

EARLY LEARNING GOAL
Physical development: Recognise the importance of keeping healthy and those things which contribute to this.

Nice teeth

Sharing the game
● Talk to your child about the importance of eating healthy foods and brushing his teeth every morning and night.
● Tell your child that you are going to play a game about it.
● Let your child look at his teeth in the mirror. Say that he has ten 'bottom' teeth and ten 'top' teeth, and that you are going to make a model of his mouth together.
● Make a horseshoe shape with Blu-Tack, approximately the size of your child's mouth. Press this on to the plate.

● Let your child count out ten mints or pieces of card. (Stress that the mints are special and only for the model, not for eating!)
● Ask your child to press the 'bottom' teeth into the Blu-Tack – four horizontally to represent 'molars' (chewing teeth) and six vertically.
● Make another horseshoe shape and ask your child to stick in ten 'top' teeth.
● Help your child to attach the 'top' teeth to the 'bottom' teeth.

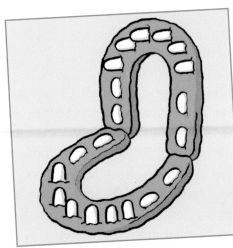

● Place the teeth in front of your child, facing away from him, and show him how to brush the teeth with the toothbrush using a gentle 'scrubbing' action.

Taking it further
● Find out together about the African crocodile that lets small birds into its mouth to clean its teeth by finding worms and insects between them.

LEARNING OPPORTUNITY
● To practise using a tissue or handkerchief.

YOU WILL NEED
Tissues or handkerchiefs.

 STEPPING STONE
Show some understanding that good practices with regard to exercise, eating, sleeping and hygiene can contribute to good health.

 EARLY LEARNING GOAL
Physical development: Recognise the importance of keeping healthy and those things which contribute to this.

Blow that nose!

Sharing the game
● Talk to your child about why she should try to 'catch her sneezes' in a tissue or handkerchief.
● Explain that we must try to always have a tissue or handkerchief, and to remember where we keep it!
● Give your child a tissue or handkerchief to put in a pocket or under her cuff ready for the game.
● Tell your child that our noses feel itchy when we are going to sneeze, and that this is when we should quickly take out our tissue or handkerchief, ready to 'catch' the sneeze.
● Sing this song together, taking out your tissue or handkerchief when you pretend to feel 'itchy' in your noses. Pretend to sneeze into your tissue or handkerchief:

Ring-o-ring-o-roses
We feel itchy in our noses
Atishoo, Atishoo
Let's catch that sneeze!

● Talk about 'runny' noses, and how we should always try to wipe our noses when this happens.

● Ask your child to put the back of one hand underneath her nostrils and to blow down her nose, keeping her lips closed. Tell her that she will feel 'a little wind' on her hand.
● Once your child can do this, show her how to blow down her nose, while gently 'squeezing' her nostrils with a tissue or handkerchief at the same time.

Taking it further
● Explain to an older child about how, a long time ago, people made each other very ill because they did not use handkerchiefs or have tissues, and did not know about germs.

LEARNING OPPORTUNITY
● To practise fastening buttons.

YOU WILL NEED
A pillow; small cushion; adult's and child's soft cardigan with large, easily managed buttons.

 STEPPING STONE
Show willingness to tackle problems and enjoy self-chosen challenges.

 EARLY LEARNING GOAL
Personal, social and emotional development: Dress and undress independently and manage their own personal hygiene.

All buttoned up!

Sharing the game
● Lay a pillow lengthways on the floor.
● Encourage your child to kneel at the foot of the pillow, and kneel behind him.
● 'Dress' the pillow in the adult's cardigan, so that it is facing away from your child.
● Invite your child to try unbuttoning and buttoning the cardigan. Talk him through the process, guiding his hands from behind, if necessary.
● Let your child stand up, put on the adult's cardigan and try managing the buttons.
● When your child is gaining confidence with the adult-sized buttons, ask him to sit on the floor and put a small cushion, 'dressed' in the child's cardigan on his knee. Ensure that the cushion is facing away from him, and provide assistance if necessary.
● Prop up the cushion in front of your child's chest and see if he can manage the buttons like this.
● Ask your child to put the cardigan on and encourage him to fasten and unfasten it.
● If he can manage this, place the small cushion on his knees, and 'dress' it in a small-buttoned item such as a school shirt. Ask your child to practise buttoning it up this way, then with the cushion

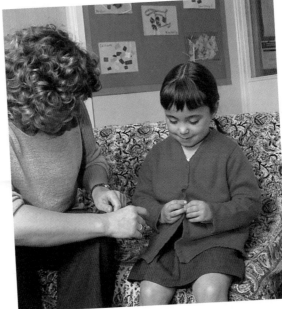

propped upright.
● Role-play dressing-up clothes, such as a sparkly magician's waistcoat, can provide an incentive for your child to master the buttoning even though they may have small buttons.

Taking it further
● Use an egg-timer to see how many clothes your child can join together by buttoning each item into a buttonhole of the next item.

Zip tricks

Sharing the game
● Ask your child to sit cross-legged on the floor and sit behind her.
● Place the adult's jacket, unzipped, over your child's knees, with the jacket facing away from her.
● Invite your child to say how she thinks that the zip works.
● Give your child a magnifying glass and look at how the teeth 'slot' into each other's spaces.

● Slowly show your child how to push the 'slider' to the end of the zip, and how to engage the two sides together.
● Give your child her own unzipped jacket to practise with when sitting on the floor (with the jacket facing away from her). Then let her put the jacket on while standing up and see if she can manage it.
● To help your child to manage narrow open-ended zips with small, 'fiddly' fasteners, roughly cut a zip from a discarded item of clothing, leaving a strip of material approximately 4cm wide on each side of the zip. Place a ruler underneath the 'slider' side of the zip, flush with the end, and secure it down the outer edge with sticky tape. This provides stability while your child practises 'clicking in' the other side of the zip.

Taking it further
● If your child's 'slider' has a hole, let her 'personalise' it by threading tinsel or a small key-chain toy through it.

LEARNING OPPORTUNITY
● To put on socks, tights and gloves.

YOU WILL NEED
A pair of adult's and child's socks and tights; pair of adult's and child's gloves.

STEPPING STONE
Pretend that one object represents another, especially when objects have characteristics in common.

EARLY LEARNING GOAL
Creative development: Use their imagination in art and design, music, dance, imaginative and role-play and stories.

Animal feet and hands

Sharing the game
Socks
● Sit barefoot on the floor next to your child and ask him to copy as you put your hand into a sock (with the heel underneath) to make 'Sammy Snake'.
● Show your child how to make Sammy's mouth very wide by putting your other hand inside, then pulling your hands away from each other, to stretch the sock's opening.
● Put your foot inside, pull up the sock, and repeat with the other foot.

● When your child has done this, ask him to remove his socks and to put them on without watching you. Sit behind him with your legs outstretched on either side of him, and gently guide him as necessary.
● Make up stories about 'Sammy Snake'.

Gloves
● Give yourself and your child a pair of gloves and ask him to copy you.
● Make your hand into a 'dog's head' and say:
  Dog's nose in first *(slide first three fingers into glove)*
  Then its ear *(slide thumb)*
  Now its mouth *(slide little finger)*
  Right down here!
  Pull the glove open with your other hand to allow thumb and little finger to be slid inside.

Taking it further
● Let your child put a pair of old gloves or socks on his hands and polish his shoes.

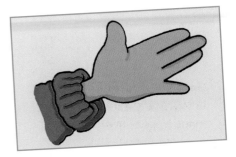

YOU WILL NEED
An adult's belt with a large, plain buckle; child's belt; adult's and child's shoes with buckles.

THINK FIRST!
Always stress to your child the importance of never putting belts near to her neck. Do not leave her to play with belts unsupervised.

STEPPING STONE
Show willingness to tackle problems and enjoy self-chosen challenges.

EARLY LEARNING GOAL
Personal, social and emotional development: Dress and undress independently and manage their own personal hygiene.

Belts and buckles

Sharing the game
● Put an adult's belt around yourself and ask your child to try to fasten it, helping her as necessary.
● Give your child her own belt to put on and encourage her to try fastening it.
● Show your child the shoe buckles. Point out that although belt buckles are usually bigger, they fasten exactly the same way as shoe buckles.

● To practise the skills involved in fastening right shoe buckles, hand your child your belt so that she is holding the buckle in her left hand, and threading the belt with her right hand.
● Let her hold the buckle in her right hand to practise left shoe buckles.
● Provide your child with a pair of adult's shoes, facing away from her, to practise with, then encourage her to try to fasten her own shoe buckles.

Taking it further
● Help your child to manage very small buckles by sliding an old watch with a buckle strap on to a kitchen-roll tube. Stand the tube in a plastic mug and pack around with toilet paper. Ask your child to try to unfasten and fasten the buckle.
● Help an older child to try to fasten her own watch with one hand. Show her how to hold her wrist by resting on her thigh.

LEARNING OPPORTUNITY
● To tie shoelaces.

YOU WILL NEED
A pair of adult's tights; scissors; cardboard carton.

 STEPPING STONE Engage in activities requiring hand–eye co-ordination.

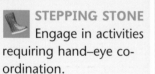 **EARLY LEARNING GOAL**
Physical development: Handle tools, objects, construction and malleable materials safely and with increasing control.

We love laces

Sharing the game

● Cut the legs off a pair of tights and knot each one at the open end.
● Create two holes in the top of the cardboard carton, approximately 10cm apart. Make each hole large enough for one leg of the tights to be pulled through.
● Push one leg through each of the holes (toes first).
● Using the tights as giant shoelaces, slowly demonstrate the process of tying them.
● Break this down into small steps and adapt your movements if you are right-handed and your child is left-handed, or vice versa.
● Kneel directly behind your child and gently guide his hands, as you talk him through each stage.

Taking it further

● If your child likes to sit on the floor and tie his laces with his feet at a right angle to his legs, help him to practise tying laces from this angle by tying the tights to two chair or table legs. Let him sit on the floor and practise tying the tights as you talk him through the steps as necessary.
● Encourage your child to tie other children's aprons for them.
● Give your child some plain paper, a hole-punch and two pieces of coloured string. Let him punch two columns of holes and thread the string, perhaps in a crisscross, and tie a bow at the bottom.

LEARNING OPPORTUNITY
● To learn to use a knife and fork.

YOU WILL NEED
Play dough (see recipe, right); two child-sized knives and forks (or plastic picnic knives and forks); two plastic plates.

THINK FIRST!
Be aware of other cultures in which fingers or chopsticks are used to eat instead of knives and forks. Make sure that your child is not allergic to the play-dough ingredients.

STEPPING STONE
Understand that equipment and tools have to be used safely.

★ **EARLY LEARNING GOAL**
Physical development: Handle tools, objects, construction and malleable materials safely and with increasing control.

Cut it up!

Recipe for play dough
4 cupfuls of plain flour
2 cupfuls of salt
2 cupfuls of oil
2 cupfuls of water (with a little food colouring), added gradually to the other ingredients.

Sharing the game
● Decide with your child which 'food' you are going to make with the play dough, for example, large tomatoes, carrots, potatoes, sausages and so on.

● Stress to your child the safe handling of knives and that she should not put them in her mouth or near to her eyes.
● When the 'food' is ready, put it on your plate and slowly pretend to eat it, talking through what you are doing, for example, 'I've just pierced the sausage with my fork to hold it still. Now I'm cutting a slice, but I never put my knife in my mouth!'.
● Sit behind your child as she pretends to eat from her own plate, and gently guide her hands as you give another running commentary using her name.

Taking it further
● Give your child real food appropriate for her to practise using a knife and fork, for example, a peeled banana, fish fingers, baby carrots and so on.
● Encourage your child to make table mats for herself and other family members. Let her draw a large knife, fork and spoon on to each mat and decorate them with drawings or cut-out pictures. Cover the mats with transparent plastic or, if possible, arrange for them to be laminated. Let your child lay appropriate cutlery on the mats for herself and for anyone else who is going to sit at the table to eat.

STEPPING STONE Match some shapes by recognising similarities and orientation.

 EARLY LEARNING GOAL Mathematical development: Use everyday words to describe position.

Not quite right!

Sharing the game
● Show your child the garments and hold them appropriately to demonstrate the meaning of upside-down and back-to-front. Then talk about inside-out and turn the garments accordingly.

● Tell your child that you will now put the fleece on, but might 'not get it quite right', in which case your child should say, 'Not quite right!'.
● Put the fleece on sometimes correctly, and sometimes not. When your child says, 'Not quite right!', ask, 'Why? What's wrong?'. Encourage him to use the three terms.
● Repeat the game with the hat.
● Ask your child to put the fleece on the correct way and then the wrong way, and to look at himself in the mirror (if available).
● When your child is wearing the fleece incorrectly, pretend that you cannot work out what is wrong and encourage him to tell you.
● Repeat the game with the hat.
● If your child enjoys the idea of 'points', award yourselves a point for each wrong feature that you both manage, for example, 'upside-down fleece' equals one point; 'upside-down and back-to-front fleece' equals two points, and so on.

Taking it further
● Cut out pictures of clothes from catalogues and magazines with your child and stick them on to paper. Ask your child to add body parts to make the clothes appear as if they are being worn upside-down or back-to-front.

CAN I HELP?

Mum is shaken awake at 5.30am on Mother's Day morning to receive her breakfast tray, lovingly prepared by four-year-old Calum, watched over by his big sister. The tray contains a cup of water, a slice of bread lavishly spread with jam, a whole lemon and a cupcake. In a yoghurt pot, there are two wilting dandelions, picked in secrecy the previous afternoon. Mum could not be more delighted if she were staying in a grand hotel, and Calum and his sister burst with pride! The development of children's self-esteem is inextricably linked with their social and emotional development, since the discovery of one's self is achieved by positive interaction with others.

KITCHEN CLEVER

Between the ages of three and four, children develop manual dexterity and competence in hand–eye co-ordination. Food preparation is an ideal context for practising these skills. From the age of four, children will benefit from talking about what they need to assemble for a recipe, and by the age of five, they should be able to read and write simple recipes with assistance.

How you can help

● Let your child practise using a wide range of safe kitchen tools, such as a lemon squeezer or melon baller, and techniques such as pouring, mixing, rolling, rubbing in pastry, kneading, using a 'pincer' movement to sprinkle herbs, and so on.

● Take your child to multicultural food supermarkets and buy utensils such as a Chinese soup bowl and spoon.
● Let your child mix fruit punches and milkshakes using a hand whisk.
● Help your child to make a simple family recipe book, using a photo album with plastic-covered pages. Add drawings and photographs of floury faces and satisfied guests at the table!
● Always introduce to your child your own rules regarding kitchen safety.

AROUND THE HOUSE

At the age of three, children develop enormously through domestic role-play, pretending to carry out all the 'grown-up' jobs that they see you do. Between the ages of three and four, they can be heard talking through their play, gradually starting to include others and the beginnings of imaginary events, often involving the knowledge of 'grown-ups' jobs'.

How you can help

● Encourage your child to help you with real tasks such as dusting and polishing.
● Even if you have a dishwasher, give your child a washing-up bowl of soapy water, dish cloth and tea towel to wash and dry unbreakable cups and plates.
● Give your child a lightweight vegetable rack on castors and let him pretend to be a 'delivery person' delivering his toys to their correct place.
● Ask your child how he would like to order items in his chest of drawers. Label them with pictures (from children's clothes catalogues) or words.

LOOKING AFTER THEIR WORLD

Your three-year-old is highly suggestible to your attitudes and actions regarding living things and the environment. Between the ages of four and five, he is fascinated by the similarities, differences, patterns and changes in the natural world around him.

How you can help

● Give your child responsibilities for special tasks such as watering plants.
● Try not to pass on any squeamishness that you may have such as for worms, snails and so on.
● Provide a plastic magnifying glass and convey a respect for nature by telling your child that minibeasts should be observed, ideally, only outside, but if they are brought inside, it should be for a very short time only, as these creatures will feel unhappy inside.
● Many five-year-olds enjoy 'collections', for example, shells, stones and so on. If possible, keep them in a plastic multi-compartmental screw-and-nail cabinet (available from DIY stores).
● Visit a favourite tree regularly with your child to notice the changes, and take a photograph each season of yourselves standing underneath it.

SHARING AND CARING

Your three-year-old will not share consistently without your prompting. By the age of four, he will need less prompting because he will be starting to be able to see things from another's point of view. Disputes will still, of course, occur, but he is now starting to try to sort them out with words.

How you can help

● Encourage your child to have lots of pretend 'parties' and 'picnics' to develop sharing, 'One for you, one for you and one for me!'.
● Ensure that your child takes turns to let others be in charge.
● Use a timer to ensure fair play when your child is taking turns with another child to play with a toy.

NEVER MIND!

Three-year-olds feel a sense of embarrassment or shame if they do something 'wrong'. By the age of four, this awareness develops into feelings of empathy for others in a predicament. Three- to four-year-olds respond well when decisions are explained clearly with reasons given. Four- to five-year-olds enjoy making plans and gathering together what they need to carry out an idea.

How you can help

● Encourage your child to say 'sorry' by telling him stories about mistakes that you made when you were little and how you said 'sorry'.

● Use glove puppets to reinforce to your child how to say 'sorry'.
● Prevent moments of confrontation and firmly offer, perhaps, two options.
● Keep things needed for a special 'project' that your child is doing in a plastic 'work tidy' (available from supermarkets).

The games featured in the first half of this chapter focus on practical activities that children love to do around the house and garden. These bring pleasure and satisfaction to themselves, as they become aware of their developing skills and of the delight in making other people happy, and to others.

The second half of the chapter centres on games that develop social skills such as listening, being flexible to change, sharing, thinking positively of others and dealing with 'disagreements' – all necessary for emotional resilience. Most of the activities relate to the Personal, social and emotional development Area of the Early Learning Goals.

● To use simple kitchen tools.

YOU WILL NEED
Six cream crackers; cream cheese; yellow pepper*; lemon*; water; sugar; banana or yellow melon; blunt knife or melon baller; sharp knife (adult use); teaspoon; two paper plates or two six-section bun tins; two transparent plastic cups; lemon squeezer; plastic jug.

 THINK FIRST!
Be aware of any food allergies or dietary requirements.
*Items marked with an asterisk are to be cut by an adult.

 STEPPING STONE
Engage in activities requiring hand–eye co-ordination.

★ **EARLY LEARNING GOAL**
Physical development: Handle tools, objects, construction and malleable materials safely and with increasing control.

Colour picnics

Sharing the game
● Tell your child that you are going to use real kitchen utensils to make a 'yummy yellow picnic'.
● Show your child how to spread the cream crackers with cream cheese and put them on the plates or in the bun tins.
● Wash and dice the pepper, and let your child put it on the crackers.
● Make the lemonade. Cut the lemon in half and encourage your child to use the squeezer.
● Help your child to pour the juice into the jug, add water and a tiny amount of sugar, and stir, then let your child pour the lemonade into the cups.
● For the dessert, ask your child to cut the banana into six slices with the blunt knife, or show him how to scoop out six balls of melon with the melon baller. Add these to the plates or bun tins.

● Encourage your child to help you to make other 'colour picnics' using cream cheese on crackers with the following toppings, desserts and drinks:
Orange: satsuma segments topping; orange-melon balls; orange juice.
Red: diced red pepper topping*; sliced red apple*; red-grape juice.
White: plain cream cheese topping; scoop of vanilla ice-cream; milk.
Green: sliced cucumber topping*; sliced green apple*; apple juice.

Taking it further
● Whenever possible, let your child practise using a variety of non-dangerous kitchen utensils such as a rotary or balloon egg whisk, rolling-pin, revolving pastry cutter, potato masher, ice-cream scoop and so on.

● To put socks into pairs.

YOU WILL NEED
An old table-cloth or
sheet; wide variety of
children's socks in
distinctive colours and
designs.

STEPPING STONE
Notice and
comment on patterns.

**EARLY LEARNING
GOAL**
Knowledge and
understanding of the
world: Look closely at
similarities, differences,
patterns and change.

Match the socks

Sharing the game
● Tell your child that this game will really help you to get an
important job done.
● Spread the table-cloth or sheet on the floor, put the pile of socks in
the middle and divide the socks equally between you.
● Encourage your child to do this by playing 'One for you, one for
me'. Then hold up a sock each. If the socks match, say, 'Snap!'. The
first person to say, 'Snap!' wins the pair.

● Help your child to fold the
top of one sock over the other
to keep them together, and to
put the pair to one side.
● If the socks that you hold
do not match, lie them side
by side in a 'spares line', to
the side of both of you. Keep
adding non-matching socks
to this line.
● Each time that two non-
matching socks are held up,
both of you should look at
the 'spares line' to see if
either of you can match
your sock.
● The winner is the player
with the most pairs.

Taking it further
● When your child is adept at matching children's socks, move on to
the challenge of matching plain adults' socks in the same colour.
Explain that you must both look very carefully at the 'hidden'
patterns, and feel the different textures to make sure that the socks
are paired together correctly.
● Place drawings of family members' faces around the edge of the
table-cloth or sheet. Together, sort out mixed laundry according to
who wears the items.

LEARNING OPPORTUNITY
● To make a reminder chart about looking after pets and plants.

YOU WILL NEED
A sheet of A4 card; felt-tipped pens; hole-punch; thick wool; sticky tape; split-pin fasteners.

 THINK FIRST!
Be aware of any allergies to animal fur and plants.

 STEPPING STONE
Show care and concern for others, for living things and the environment.

EARLY LEARNING GOAL
Personal, social and emotional development: Consider the consequences of their words and actions for themselves and others.

Fed and watered

Sharing the game
● Provide your child with a sheet of A4 card and invite her to draw, down the left-hand side, pictures of any pets or plants that need looking after.
● Ask your child to punch a hole next to each picture.
● Give your child a piece of wool, approximately 40cm long, and ask her to thread it through each hole. Secure at the back with sticky tape.

● Down the right-hand side of the card, help your child to write, in random order, what the pets and plants need, for example, light, water and carrot or the names of pet food. If necessary, your child can write on top of your writing or underneath it.
● Push a split-pin fastener to the left of each word.

● Each day, as your child feeds a pet or waters a plant, ask her to stretch the wool across the card and wind it around the appropriate split-pin fastener.

Taking it further
● Photocopy the page of the current month of a large wall calendar that is divided into squares. Place it next to any plant that your child is looking after and let her colour in each square to show that she has checked her plant every day, and watered it if necessary.

LEARNING OPPORTUNITY
● To make a gift to celebrate a friend's festival.

YOU WILL NEED
A diary; empty cereal packet; scissors; tin foil; sticky tape; eight decorated fairy-cake cases; cling film.

THINK FIRST!
Be aware of any food allergies or dietary requirements.

STEPPING STONE
Have an awareness of, and show interest and enjoyment in, cultural and religious differences.

EARLY LEARNING GOAL
Personal, social and emotional development: Understand that people have different needs, views, cultures and beliefs, that need to be treated with respect.

Festival trays

Sharing the game
● Show your child the diary and look up the date of a festival that a friend might be about to celebrate.

● Cut out one large side of the cereal box to make an 'open tray' and secure with sticky tape.
● Let your child help you to cover the tray with foil and put eight decorated fairy-cake cases on the tray.
● Depending on the festival, place the following in the cake cases:

Chinese New Year – satsuma segments.

Divali (Hindu Festival of Light, also celebrated by some Sikh people) – coconut ice balls. Mix eight tablespoons of desiccated coconut and three tablespoons of condensed milk. Use the paste to make eight balls, then chill them.

Rosh Hashana (Jewish New Year) – put apple slices into seven of the cases; replace the eighth case with a plastic mousse pot containing set honey into which the apple slices can be dipped.

Eid-ul-Fitr (Muslim festival that celebrates the end of the fasting period of Ramadan) – purchase sugared almonds or ready-to-eat stoned dates.

Christmas – cover eight plain biscuits with glacé icing; draw simple outline diagrams on paper for your child to copy on to the biscuits, using writing icing, when the glacé icing is dry.
● Cover the trays with cling film.

Taking it further
● Help your child to write 'Happy Chinese New Year, Happy Divali, Shanah Tovah (Happy Jewish New Year), Eid Mubarak (Happy Eid), Merry Christmas, love from…' on a small piece of card. Punch a hole in it, thread it with ribbon and attach it to the tray.

YOU WILL NEED
An egg-timer; two 2-litre plastic bottles (thoroughly dry on the inside); half a cup of salt; small piece of stiff card; sharp scissors; sticky tape; sheet of A4 paper.

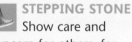

 STEPPING STONE
Show care and concern for others, for living things and the environment.

EARLY LEARNING GOAL
Personal, social and emotional development: Consider the consequences of their words and actions for themselves and others.

Tidy-up time

Sharing the game
● Show your child the egg-timer and explain how it works and why it is used.
● Tell your child that together you are going to make a giant salt-timer to use when it is time to tidy up.
● Ask your child to fold the sheet of paper in half and open it out.
● Let your child put a small amount of salt on to the paper, then use this to pour the salt carefully into a bottle. Continue until all the salt is in the bottle.
● Cut the piece of card into a disc that is the same size as the bottle necks.
● Make a small hole yourself in the centre of the disc with the two points of the closed scissors.
● Place the disc of card on top of the bottle containing the salt and secure with tape. Do not cover the hole.
● Balance the empty bottle upside-down on top of the first bottle and secure both necks with plenty of tape.
● Decide together on one main tidying-up task, for example, picking up just the toy cars and putting them in their box.
● Ask your child to upturn the timer, then together pick up the cars and try to beat the timer.
● Continue to break up the tidying-up task into several 'mini jobs', using the timer for each of them.

Taking it further
● Play a favourite song and see if you can both tidy up before the end.

LEARNING OPPORTUNITY
● To learn why we must not drop litter.

YOU WILL NEED
A small bin containing 'clean' waste paper; play bricks; 'used' floral greetings card; scissors; small-world people; four aerosol can tops.

Looking after our world

Sharing the game
● Tip the contents of the bin on to the floor.
● Explain to your child that you have done this on purpose because you want to talk about litter. Say that you will not do it again and that he should not do it, either!
● Tell your child that we should not drop litter on the floor inside our homes or in any building, nor should we do this outside.

● Suggest to your child that you build a 'street' to show what it is like with and without litter.
● Create a 'park' scene by arranging flowers, cut from the greetings card, on the floor, and surround them with a 'brick wall'.
● Arrange the small-world people along the 'street'.
● Tear up some of the waste paper into small pieces and scatter them along the 'street', including on top of the flowers.
● Point out how unpleasant it is for the small-world people to have to walk through the litter.
● Produce the aerosol lids to use as 'bins'. Talk about why we use them and, together, arrange them along the 'street'.
● Encourage your child to help you to pick up the litter and put it in the 'bins'.
● Challenge your child to say what we should do with the litter if we cannot find a bin.

Taking it further
● Encourage your child to decorate a giant, plastic plant pot to use as a litter bin.

 STEPPING STONE
Show an interest in the world in which they live.

EARLY LEARNING GOAL
Knowledge and understanding of the world: Find out about their environment, and talk about those features they like and dislike.

CAN I HELP?

LEARNING OPPORTUNITY
● To listen carefully to instructions.

YOU WILL NEED
Two toy telephones (or improvised 'mobile phones' made from play bricks); coloured play bricks; toy car; small-world person; sticky tape; plain paper; scissors; pencil.

STEPPING STONE
Respond to simple instructions.

EARLY LEARNING GOAL
Communication, language and literacy: Sustain attentive listening, responding to what they have heard by relevant comments, questions or actions.

All ears

Sharing the game

● Explain to your child that it is very important to listen carefully to instructions.

● Talk about how a doctor's receptionist must listen very carefully on the telephone to hear the names and addresses of patients.

● Tell your child that the receptionists write down the names and addresses so that they do not forget them, and then tell the doctors so that they know where to go.

● Have a street of ten 'front doors' by standing the bricks, vertically, side by side.

● Write the numbers 1 to 10 on small pieces of paper and attach them to each 'door' with sticky tape.

● Decide together on a name for your 'street'.

● Ask your child to be the 'doctor's receptionist' and give her a telephone, paper and pencil.

● Ring her on the telephone, saying that you are poorly, and ask for a doctor's visit, giving your name and address.

● Encourage your child to 'write' your name and address as you speak, using her own version of pretend writing.

● Ask your child to repeat your name and address to the small-world person (doctor).

● Let your child put the 'doctor' in the car and 'drive around' to the correct house. (If your child cannot yet recognise numbers, use the colour of the door instead.)

Taking it further

● Give your child lots of messages and real 'jobs' involving listening, for example, 'Please put the socks in the bottom drawer and bring me the blue T-shirt from the top drawer'.

LEARNING OPPORTUNITY
● To learn to be flexible about changes in expected events.

YOU WILL NEED
Two pieces of plain paper, approximately A5 size; felt-tipped pen; two fridge magnets or Blu-Tack.

STEPPING STONE
Demonstrate flexibility and adapt their behaviour to different events, social situations and changes in routine.

EARLY LEARNING GOAL
Personal, social and emotional development: Work as part of a group or class, taking turns and sharing fairly, understanding that there needs to be agreed values and codes of behaviour for groups of people, including adults and children, to work together harmoniously.

Just in case

Sharing the game
● If you think that there might be a possibility that a plan such as a visit to the park may need to be changed, for example, because of rain, help to reduce disappointment by giving your child a sense of 'ownership' about deciding on a contingency plan.
● Together, draw a very simple picture of the planned activity on the first piece of paper, and display it on the fridge door.
● Explain to your child that grown-ups often like to think of another idea, just in case the first idea is not possible.
● Ask your child to think of a 'just in case' activity.
● Write 'Just in case' across the top of the second piece of paper and together draw a picture.
● Display this next to the first picture, referring to it if necessary.

Taking it further
● Draw three small 'contingency' pictures together. Put each picture inside an empty film canister, covered with pretty paper. Invite your child to close his eyes and pick a surprise thing to do whenever necessary.
● If you have to interrupt your child because of something unexpected, try, if possible, to give a little notice, even if only a minute.

One for you, one for me

CAN I HELP?

LEARNING OPPORTUNITY
● To realise that, when sharing, people should have equal amounts.

YOU WILL NEED
Two six-section thin plastic trays such as from boxes of individual fruit pies, biscuits, egg cartons and so on, or a bun tin; 12 satsuma segments or grapes; plastic dish.

 STEPPING STONE Compare two groups of objects, saying when they have the same number.

EARLY LEARNING GOAL
Mathematical development: Use language such as 'more' or 'less' to compare two numbers.

Sharing the game
● Explain to your child that this game will show her how to share things properly.
● Ask your child to wash her hands and help you to put the satsuma segments into the dish.
● Put a tray in front of both of you. Place two satsuma segments in your child's tray and the rest in yours.
● Ask, 'Is that fair? No! I've got more than you have and you've got less than I have! We should both have the same!'.

● Replace the segments in the dish and share them again, saying, 'One for you and one for me' until all the segments are used up.
● Ask your child to count the segments in her tray and to guess how many you have.
● Say, 'Yes, that's right! Six each! We've both got the same amount of satsuma segments. Is that fair?'.
● Replace the segments in the dish and ask your child to share them out, saying, 'One for you, one for me'.

Taking it further
● Use trays containing more than six sections, such as a 12-section bun tin.
● Prepare an odd number of satsuma segments, so that there is one left over. Encourage your child to tell you what would be the fair thing to do in this situation.

● ●

Happy five

Sharing the game

● Play this game at the end of the day.
● Invite your child to tuck one of his thumbs inside the fingers of one hand.
● Do the same yourself.
● Take turns to recall things that happened during the day that made you feel happy, for example, someone saying something nice to you, someone being kind to you, or something you did or saw, heard, touched, smelled or tasted.
● Each time that one of you recalls something, put up your thumb and then one finger at a time, until both of you have raised four fingers and one thumb.

Taking it further

● Play 'Happy five memory lane' in the same way, with both of you remembering five happy things that have happened in the past, for example, on an outing, at a party, on holiday, when he was little and so on.
● When the situation arises, let your child talk about anything that may have made him feel sad. Whenever possible and appropriate, try to encourage him to think about something that he could do himself to try to make the situation better, for example, help to make or buy a cushion for Grandad's poorly back, send a toy, clothes or money from his money box to help others, or say 'sorry'.

LEARNING OPPORTUNITY
● To realise that, in resolving disputes, both sides must be heard.

YOU WILL NEED
Two teddy bears; felt-tipped pen; sticky tape.

STEPPING STONE
Initiate conversation, attend to and take account of what others say, and use talk to resolve disagreements.

EARLY LEARNING GOAL
Communication, language and literacy: Interact with others, negotiating plans and activities and taking turns in conversation.

What's the problem?

Sharing the game

● Make two balls of adhesive tape (sticky side out) and attach one to a paw of each of the bears.
● Attach the felt-tipped pen to one of the bears' paw.
● Sit the bears side by side and enact a short scenario in which the second bear deliberately takes the pen from the first bear.
● Make the first bear retrieve the pen.
● End the scenario with both bears 'in tears'.
● Tell your child that the bears would like her to help to sort out their problem, and that to do this she must let both bears say what happened.
● Say that this song will help her to remember that whenever there is an argument, both people must be asked to talk about it.
● Sing the song to the tune of 'I Hear Thunder' (Traditional).
   What's the problem? *(repeat)*
   Let's see what we can do! *(repeat)*
   First, let's hear from one of you,
   Then the other, too!
● Play the parts of both bears, each giving their version of events, for example, 'She took my pen!' and 'Well, my pen's run out!'.
● Ask your child what she thinks should be done to resolve the dispute between the bears.

Taking it further

● Place a tower of three small bricks in front of one bear. Put a fourth brick near by and make the second bear accidentally trip over it and knock down the tower. Sing the song together. Then, hear both bears' views as before and ask your child how to sort out the situation.

LEARNING OPPORTUNITY
● To learn that people's facial expressions and body language can tell us how they are feeling.

YOU WILL NEED
A mirror; cushion; adult's and child's fleece or cardigan.

STEPPING STONE
Initiate interactions with other people.

EARLY LEARNING GOAL
Personal, social and emotional development: Have a developing awareness of their own needs, views and feelings and be sensitive to the needs, views and feelings of others.

Inside feelings

Sharing the game
● Talk with your child about feeling happy, sad and cross.
● Tell your child that often other people can know what we are feeling inside by looking at the outside of our faces (expressions), and at what we do with our bodies (body language).
● Together, make happy, sad and cross expressions in the mirror and corresponding body movements.
● Explain to your child that if we can see from a person's face and body that they are not feeling happy, it is very kind to try to make them feel better.

● Ask your child how he could help someone who looked tired (get a cushion, slippers and so on), cold (get a fleece, ask a grown-up to make a warm drink), sad (give a hug and have a chat) or cross (have a chat, and say 'sorry' if necessary).
● Pretend to be tired, then cold, sad and cross.
● Ask your child to guess how you are feeling and to make you feel better, for example, by giving you the cushion.
● Continue taking turns at being the person needing comfort and the comforter.

Taking it further
● Turn off the sound on your television for a few moments, such as when an advertisement or a soap opera is showing. Ask your child how he thinks one of the people might be feeling from their facial expression and body language.

LET'S EAT

In order to develop in your child a healthy attitude towards food and eating, it is very important that the food is eaten at the end of each game and not wasted. If your child has a poor appetite, substitute small food items that you know she likes.

When playing the games, keep the emphasis on the food as the motivating 'end product' of the game, so that your child is not encouraged to 'play with' food and treat it as a toy. For this reason, all the activities, except one, are designed to be carried out as short, fun, healthy, snack-time activities, and not at main meal times.

NUMBERS ALL AROUND
Children need to be aware that numbers are used as 'labels' to identify things such as buses, cars and doors, and to help us to make things work, such as TV remote controls, microwaves and alarm clocks.

How you can help
● Point out numbers to your child whenever possible – for example, on bus and car journeys, on electrical appliances and so on – and say their names.
● Talk to your child whenever you are carrying out simple daily activities that involve numbers, and let her see you write numbers as often as possible, for example, when jotting down telephone numbers or writing shopping lists.

NUMBER SEQUENCE
This involves saying the number names in order such as 'one, two, three' and so on 'off by heart'.

How you can help
● Encourage your child to join in counting or singing aloud the number of, for example, toothbrushes in the bathroom, snails on the path and biscuits on a plate.

● Number rhymes and stories such as 'One, Two, Three, Four, Five, Once I Caught a Fish Alive' and 'Goldilocks and the Three Bears' (Traditional) are very valuable. It is very motivating to bring in your child's name in a rhyme or story.

RECOGNISING NUMBERS
This involves matching number names to the correct numerals.

How you can help
● Play 'Show me' and 'Point to' number games with your child, using number friezes, posters and books as well as very short, made-up games using plastic or wooden numerals. To begin with, separate out the numerals 1 and 2 from the rest, and use only these for some time until your child can say their names on sight. Then add the numeral 3 and so on.

NUMBER VALUE

This involves matching numbers (spoken or written) with the correct number of items in a group. To do this, your child needs to learn to count items accurately 'one at a time'.

How you can help

● Encourage your child to count slowly and to say each number name only when she touches or moves an item. Teach her this rhyme:

How do we play the counting game?
We touch when we say the number name!

● Use a plastic hors d'oeuvres dish with four or six sections to help your child to match written numerals to groups of objects. Write numbers on separate pieces of paper and put one in each section. Ask your child to put the correct number of small toys, shells, stones and so on in each section.

'LAST NUMBER' RULE

This means that when your child is asked a 'how many' question, she knows that she must count the items and say the last number counted.

How you can help

● Ask your child, for example, 'How many bricks are here?' and let her count the items. Then repeat the question. If your child understands the rule, she should say the last number straight away. If she starts counting the items again, ask guided questions to prompt her, for example, 'How many did you say? Was it five or six?'.

CONSERVATION OF NUMBER

This means that the number of items in a group does not change, even though the items may move around.

How you can help

● Count your fingers together, pointing out that it does not matter whether the fingers are 'squashed together' or 'spread out'.
● Ask your child to thread beads and to count them, both 'squashed together' and 'spread out'. Do the same with ducks floating on water in a bowl or the bath.

CALCULATING

This is about using numbers in practical situations, for example, adding two groups of items together, 'taking away' and sharing out items.

How you can help

● Encourage your child to see herself as a solver of simple problems. For example, say, 'There will be four girls and three boys at your party. How many party bags will we need?', 'There were four zebras here, but now there are only three. How many are hiding?' and 'Can you share out these honey sandwiches between your bears?'.

SHAPE, SPACE AND MEASURE

Developing understanding in this area involves children in exploring the properties of 2-D and 3-D shapes, comparing them, naming them and 'spotting' them in the environment. To develop spatial awareness, children need to handle shapes and fit them together. Understanding measure involves comparing sizes and quantities, and using time language, such as 'morning' and 'afternoon', prior to an eventual understanding of measuring time.

How you can help

● Provide plenty of opportunities for your child to build with bricks on a small scale, make models with empty food packets on a medium scale, and construct large-scale vehicles, dens and cities with cartons, cushions and so on.
● Let your child make pictures and patterns with 2-D shapes, and try to fill seed trays, for example, with different arrangements of small bricks.

● Develop your child's understanding of measure and time language by involving her in preparing meals and talking about the process by using words such as 'more', 'less', 'enough', 'how many cupfuls', 'first we…', 'then we…' and so on.
● Food provides a very enjoyable and realistic context for the development of mathematical understanding in the first eleven games of this chapter. The last three games are related to the development of communication, language and literacy skills in relation to table manners.

LEARNING
OPPORTUNITY
● To make a purchase on
a real shopping trip using
pennies.

YOU WILL NEED
Pennies; child's shopping
bag; child's easy-to-open
purse or wallet.

🥾 **STEPPING STONE**
Recognise numerals
1 to 5, then 1 to 9.

⭐ **EARLY LEARNING
GOAL**
Mathematical
development: Recognise
numerals 1 to 9.

My shopping time

Sharing the game

● In advance, look around your local food shops and supermarket for items that can be bought with pennies, for example, a bread roll, yoghurt, fruit such as a lemon or apple, the supermarket's own-brand products such as flour, bread and tins of baked beans and plum tomatoes.

● Choose a quiet shopping day, such as a Monday, and set aside time for your child's own special shopping outing, which, ideally, should not be part of your own shopping trip. Handling pennies and making a purchase herself will make shopping personally meaningful for your child.

● Before you go shopping, talk about the items that are available to buy and ask your child to choose one.

● Decide on something special to use the item for after the trip, for example, the lemon to make lemonade, the flour for fairy cakes or the tinned tomatoes to make a simple vegetable soup.

● Once your child has decided on her purchase, give her a few more pennies than she will need to put in her purse.

● At the supermarket, help your child to take a basket, if necessary, then to find the item.

● Look at the price label and ask your child if she knows the number.

● Help your child to complete the purchase, for example, by finding the 'basket only' aisle of a supermarket, and by counting out her pennies.

Taking it further

● Play 'Shops' at home with items priced in pennies.

LET'S EAT

Dotty spots

LEARNING OPPORTUNITY
● To recognise groups of up to three items.

YOU WILL NEED
Six small savoury crackers (any shape); cream cheese; raisins; two blunt knives; three plastic plates; dice; paper; felt-tipped pen; sticky tape; scissors.

THINK FIRST!
Be aware of any food allergies or dietary requirements.

STEPPING STONE
Recognise groups with one, two or three objects.

EARLY LEARNING GOAL
Mathematical development: Count reliably up to 10 everyday objects.

Sharing the game
● Draw three small sad faces on to the paper (to fit the sides of the dice).
● Cut the faces out and stick them on top of the four, five and six dots of the dice.
● Give yourself and your child three crackers each and spread the cream cheese on.
● Put one, two and three raisins on each cracker to look like the dots on a dice.
● Put all the crackers on one plate and take an empty plate each.
● Take turns to throw the dice. According to the throw, take a matching cracker from the plate each. Miss a turn on the throw of a 'sad' face, or if you already have the cracker to match the number thrown.
● The first person to assemble three crackers with one, two and three raisins, lined up in the correct order, is the winner.

Taking it further
● To help your child to recognise different arrangements of up to three items, draw groups of two and three dots using a 'pattern' different from a traditional dice.
● Take six raisins each and put them on your plates. Take turns to throw the dice and eat the number of raisins matching the number of dots on the dice. The first person to eat all their raisins in the winner.

LEARNING OPPORTUNITY
● To match number names to strides.

YOU WILL NEED
A doormat; five plastic plates; 15 small food items such as satsuma segments; sound maker such as a drum or rattle.

THINK FIRST!
Beware of any food allergies or dietary requirements.

STEPPING STONE
Count actions or objects that cannot be moved.

EARLY LEARNING GOAL
Mathematical development: Count reliably up to 10 everyday objects (or 'events').

Giant footsteps

Sharing the game
● Put the mat on the floor and the five plates at intervals of approximately one of your child's strides in a vertical line in front, and slightly to the left, of the mat to look like a ladder.
● Put one satsuma segment on the first plate, two on the second and so on.
● Ask your child to stand on the mat and to listen to how many beats you are going to make on the sound maker. Encourage her to make the same number of 'giant footsteps'.
● Make two beats slowly and help your child to make two strides, as far as the second plate.
● Let your child eat the satsuma segments, then ask her to return to the mat to continue the game, until all the food is eaten.

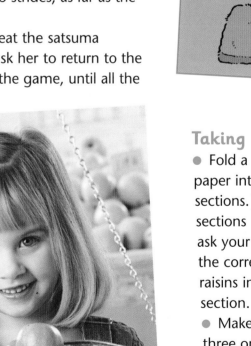

Taking it further
● Fold a sheet of A4 paper into four sections. Number the sections 1 to 4 and ask your child to place the correct number of raisins in each section.
● Make one, two, three or four beats on a drum and ask your child to count the beats and eat the matching number of raisins.

LEARNING OPPORTUNITY
● To match numbers with groups of objects.

YOU WILL NEED
Two digestive biscuits; packet of coloured birthday candles with matching holders; small tube of writing icing.

THINK FIRST!
Be aware of any food allergies or dietary requirements. Although no candles are lit in this game, use it as an opportunity to talk about the need for safety when using candles.

STEPPING STONE
Count out up to six objects from a larger group.

EARLY LEARNING GOAL
Mathematical development: Count reliably up to 10 everyday objects.

Happy birthday!

Sharing the game
● Help your child to put the coloured candles in the matching candle holders.
● Ask your child how old he is and how many candles he will need for a special birthday 'cake'.
● Write your child's age number on a digestive biscuit with the writing icing. (Alternatively, write the number with a felt-tipped pen on a small piece of paper and put it in the middle of the biscuit.)
● Spread out all the candles in their holders on the table and ask your child to take the correct number of candles and put them around his 'cake' (using the pre-existing holes in the biscuit).
● Ask your child to think of a pet or toy that he can make a 'cake' for and put on the correct number of candles.
● Sing 'Happy Birthday' and eat the cakes.

Taking it further
● Encourage your child to make age badges for his teddy bears using card, felt-tipped pens and scissors. Let him stick a badge on each bear, with sticky tape and make a 'cake' for them.
● Encourage your child to create a card shop with used birthday cards showing age numbers.

LEARNING OPPORTUNITY
● To work out how many cheese cubes are necessary for 'mice families'.

YOU WILL NEED
A chair; piece of material such as a table-cloth; two empty cereal packets; scissors; 15 cubes of cheese; five plastic plates; felt-tipped pen.

THINK FIRST! Be aware of any food allergies or dietary requirements.

STEPPING STONE Compare two groups of objects, saying when they have the same number.

EARLY LEARNING GOAL Mathematical development: Use language such as 'more' or 'less' to compare two numbers.

Mouse house party

Sharing the game
● Put a cube of cheese on one plate, two on the second and so on.
● Cover the chair with the material to create a 'dark mouse hole'.
● Cut open the cereal packets and lay them flat.
● Draw one mouse, a pair of mice, a group of three mice, and so on up to five.

● Draw a circle around each 'family' and cut it out. Put one of the discs under the chair.
● Encourage your child to crawl inside the 'mouse hole' and count how many mice there are in the family. Ask her how many cubes of cheese the family would need to have 'one each'.
● Invite your child to find the correct plate and to crawl back inside to bring out the family.
● Ask your child to put a cube of cheese next to each mouse to make sure that there are enough cubes. Say, for example, 'Four mice, four cubes! That is the same number, so the mice can have one each!'.
● Put your ear next to each 'mouse' and say that they have just said thank you for the cheese, but are not hungry just now and would like your child to eat it!

Taking it further
● Use the mice and cubes of cheese to pose very simple adding and subtraction problems to your child, for example, 'How many cubes will we need for this family and that family altogether?', or 'This family has eaten only two cubes. How many cubes are left?'.

Still the same!

Sharing the game

- Draw a brown, leafless tree on both sheets of paper, one for you and one for your child.
- Talk about how leaves turn brown in autumn and fall off the trees.
- Together, put three cornflakes (autumn leaves) on your trees.
- Ask your child to count his 'leaves'.
- Say, 'Yes, that's right, two over there and one down here. Two leaves and one more leaf makes three leaves altogether!'.

- Put your tree next to your child's tree.
- Point out to your child that although your 'leaf' arrangements are different, you both have three leaves.
- Gently blow your 'leaves' off your tree, on to the 'ground' at the bottom of your sheet.
- Say, 'Now my leaves have fallen off the tree. Look, they are on the ground side by side in a line, and there are still the same number – three!'.
- Ask your child how many leaves there would be on the ground in his picture if the leaves fell off his tree.

Taking it further

- Help your child to understand the 'last number' rule (the last number spoken gives the total number of items) by making a 'pile' of leaves (up to five).
- Ask your child to count the leaves in the 'pile'.
- Say, 'I'm sorry, I didn't hear you properly. How many leaves did you say there were?'.
- Encourage your child to say the last number straight away, without counting from one again.

LET'S EAT

LEARNING OPPORTUNITY

● To eat a small quantity of purple grapes and green grapes and say how many grapes have been eaten altogether.

YOU WILL NEED

Six purple grapes; six green grapes; large plastic plate; two six-egg boxes; two sheets of A4 paper; scissors; purple felt-tipped pen; green felt-tipped pen.

THINK FIRST!
Be aware of any food allergies or dietary requirements.

STEPPING STONE
Find the total number of items in two groups by counting all of them.

EARLY LEARNING GOAL
Mathematical development: Begin to relate addition to combining two groups of objects and subtraction to 'taking away'.

Purple and green

Sharing the game

● Fold the sheets of A4 paper into four and cut out the sections.
● Write the numbers 1 to 3 in purple on each of three sections.
● Repeat using the green felt-tipped pen.
● Make two 'piles' of numbers from 1 to 3, one in purple and one in green, side by side, number-side facing down.
● Put the washed grapes on to the plate.
● Take turns with your child to pick two numbers each (one purple and one green), replacing the numbers each time in the 'pile'.
● Put the corresponding number and colour of grape(s) in your egg-boxes (purple grapes on the top row, and green grapes on the bottom row).
● Encourage your child to verbalise her arrangement of grapes, for example, 'Three purple grapes and two green grapes make five grapes altogether!'.
● The winner is the first player to fill their egg-box.

Taking it further

● Use two empty trays from a small chocolate box with the corresponding number of purple and green grapes.
● Practise the concept of 'one more' by putting four purple grapes and four green grapes on the plate.
● Have one 'pile' of numbers and take turns to turn over a number.
● Whatever number is chosen, work out what 'one more' would be, and take the corresponding number of grapes from the plate.
● Say the rhyme 'One Elephant' (see page 126).

LEARNING OPPORTUNITY
● To develop an understanding of subtraction by using breadstick 'sausages' in a pan.

YOU WILL NEED
A breadstick; bread knife; frying pan; white cotton.

THINK FIRST!
Be aware of any food allergies or dietary requirements.

STEPPING STONE
Sometimes show confidence and offer solutions to problems.

EARLY LEARNING GOAL
Mathematical development: Begin to relate addition to combining two groups of objects, and subtraction to 'taking away'.

Sizzle, sizzle, sizzle

Sharing the game
● Cut the breadstick into five small pieces (to represent sausages) with the bread knife.
● Tie a piece of cotton, approximately 20cm long, around each piece.
● Put the 'sausages' in the frying pan.
● Say the rhyme 'Five Fat Sausages' (see page 126), adapted from 'Ten Fat Sausages' (Traditional).
● As you recite the rhyme, encourage your child to use his fingers to work out how many sausages are left after each 'Bang!'. Let him pull a 'sausage' up in the air, holding the cotton, to indicate that the sausage has burst and 'popped' into the air.
● Encourage your child to try to work out himself how many sausages are left, by using his fingers, before looking in the pan to check.

Taking it further
● Make a bib with a pocket for a teddy bear from a large paper handkerchief or piece of kitchen roll. Attach the bib to the bear with sticky tape.
● Put five 'sausages' on a plate in front of the bear. Encourage your child to pretend that the bear is 'eating' the sausages one by one. As

each sausage is eaten, hide it inside the pocket and ask your child how many sausages are left each time.
● Place three sausages on a plate and ask your child to close his eyes while you remove a sausage. Ask him to open his eyes, look at the remaining sausages and work out how many you have taken. Repeat using four, then five sausages.

● To learn to match and name 2-D shapes by preparing sandwiches.

YOU WILL NEED
Six slices of bread; blunt knife; soft margarine; easy-to-spread sandwich filling such as cheese spread, mashed banana, and tuna and mayonnaise; different-shaped biscuit cutters such as a circle, square, rectangle, triangle, heart and diamond; tray; bread board.

THINK FIRST!
Be aware of any food allergies or dietary requirements.

STEPPING STONE
Match some shapes by recognising similarities and orientation.

EARLY LEARNING GOAL
Mathematical development: Use language such as 'circle' or 'bigger' to describe the shape and size of solids and flat shapes.

Yummy picnic shapes

Sharing the game

● Help your child to spread the margarine on the slices of bread using the blunt knife and bread board.
● Encourage your child to use the cutters to cut out two identical shapes from each slice of bread, using a different shape for each slice.
● Together, arrange a row of one of each cut-out bread shape on the tray.
● Ask your child to close her eyes.
● Hold her forefinger and help her to feel around the outer edge of each bread shape. Use words such as 'straight sides', 'four corners', 'curved', 'round' and so on, to encourage her to name any of the shapes.
● Invite your child to put the second set of matching bread shapes underneath the first row of shapes on the tray.

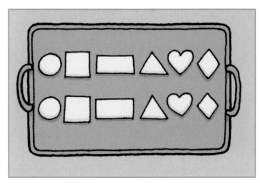

● Invite your child to spread a little filling on each of the shapes on the top row.
● Encourage your child to put each of the shapes from the bottom row on top of the matching shape in the top row, to complete the sandwiches.

Taking it further

● Describe each sandwich shape for your child to guess, for example, 'It is the same shape as a wheel', 'If it were metal, you could play it' and so on.

LEARNING OPPORTUNITY
● To practise using height language by pretending to grow lettuce plants.

YOU WILL NEED
A little gem lettuce; kitchen roll; bread board; child's watering can; two soft-toy animals (one smaller than the other).

STEPPING STONE
Order two items by length or height.

EARLY LEARNING GOAL
Mathematical development: Use language such as 'circle' or 'bigger' to describe the shape and size of solids and flat shapes.

Tall and taller

Sharing the game
● Pull the leaves of the lettuce apart. Wash and pat them dry with the kitchen roll.
● Make up a very simple 'story' about two of your child's soft toys who decide to grow a lettuce plant each.
● Say that the first animal (the small one) forgot to water her lettuce and that it only grew two leaves.
● Ask your child to arrange two lettuce leaves side by side on the bread board, to represent the plant.

● Say that the other animal (the large one) remembered to water his plant often, so that it grew two leaves, then it grew four leaves and then it grew six leaves.
● Let your child pretend to be the second animal 'watering' the plant with the empty watering can.
● Encourage your child to arrange six leaves in a 'tall' plant.
● Ask your child, 'Which is the short plant?', 'Which is the tall plant?', 'Which is taller?' and 'Which is shorter?'.
● Invite your child to curl up like the small animal and to eat his short lettuce plant, and then to stretch up like the big animal, and eat his tall lettuce plant.

Taking it further
● Cut up a breadstick into a 'small', 'medium' and 'long' pieces, with a bread knife. Alternatively, use carrot or celery sticks.
● With your child, 'feed' each piece to three teddy bears – small 'Baby Bear', middle-sized 'Mummy Bear', and tall 'Daddy Bear'.

LEARNING OPPORTUNITY
● To develop an understanding of 'heavy' and 'light', using a home-made coat-hanger scale.

YOU WILL NEED
A crescent-shaped coat-hanger; string; sharp-pointed scissors (adult use); two large, wide margarine pots; 'heavy' and 'light' fruit and vegetables.

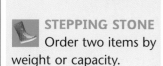

STEPPING STONE
Order two items by weight or capacity.

EARLY LEARNING GOAL
Mathematical development: Use language such as 'greater', 'smaller', 'heavier' or 'lighter' to compare quantities.

Up and down

Sharing the game
● Pierce three holes in each of the margarine pots.
● Thread a loop of string, approximately 40cm long, through each hole and make a knot at the end.
● Knot the three loops together on each pot, and attach both pots to the ends of the coat-hanger to create a pair of scales.

● Put the hook of the coat-hanger on a door knob.
● Arrange different pairs of fruit and vegetables that are heavy and light, for example, a potato and sprout, or a melon and a strawberry.
● Invite your child to hold out both hands to feel, in turn, the pairs of fruit or vegetables, and to say which is heavier and which is lighter.
● Ask your child to check her guess by putting each pair on the 'scales', noting which side goes down and which goes up. Encourage her to explain why this happens.

Taking it further
● Give your child a satsuma or carrot in one hand, and three satsumas or carrots in the other.
● Ask your child to say which hand has the heavier 'load' and to predict which side of the coat-hanger will go down, depending on whether one or three items are placed inside one of the margarine pots.
● Put the same number of items in each of your child's hands to demonstrate that they feel the 'same' weight.
● Ask your child to put them on the scales and see how they balance.
● Place four items in one margarine pot and one item in the other.
● Find out how many more items will make the scales balance.

LEARNING OPPORTUNITY
● To practise offering food to other people, and to say 'please' and 'thank you'.

YOU WILL NEED
Two plates; small tray; two healthy snacks; tea towel; clip-on bow ties or paper doily and hair clips; waistcoat or 'ball gown'.

THINK FIRST!
Be aware of any food allergies or dietary requirements, and that, in some cultures, 'please' and 'thank you' are not as commonly used as in English.

STEPPING STONE
Use language for an increasing range of purposes.

EARLY LEARNING GOAL
Communication, language and literacy: Speak clearly and audibly with confidence and control and show awareness of the listener, for example, by their use of conventions such as greetings, 'please' and 'thank you'.

Grown-ups' parties

Sharing the game
● Tell your child that at some grown-ups' parties, waiters or waitresses carry trays of food around.
● Dress your child either as a waiter or waitress by using a knotted tea towel as an apron, and a bow tie or a paper doily and some hair clips (for a cap).
● Let a boy party guest wear a waistcoat, and a girl party guest wear a 'ball gown'.
● Put a choice of two healthy snacks on the tray, for example, apple and banana slices, or cucumber and carrot sticks.
● Ask the 'waiter' to present the tray to the 'guests' saying 'Would you like… or …?'.
● Encourage the guests to reply with, 'Yes, please', followed by, 'Thank you' or 'No, thank you'.

Taking it further
● Help your child, as a 'guest', to ask politely for more, by saying 'Could I have another…, please?'.

LEARNING OPPORTUNITY
● To choose and serve food, learning to say 'please' and 'thank you'.

YOU WILL NEED
A plastic, four or six-sectioned hors d'oeuvres dish; 'serving' cutlery, for example, spoons, forks, tongs, hinged salad servers, ice-cream scoops and so on.

THINK FIRST!
Be aware of any food allergies or dietary requirements.

STEPPING STONE
Use language for an increasing range of purposes.

EARLY LEARNING GOAL
Communication, language and literacy: Speak clearly and audibly with confidence and control and show awareness of the listener, for example by their use of conventions such as greetings, 'please' and 'thank you'.

Caring and sharing

Sharing the game

● Occasionally, consider putting the different kinds of food for a family meal on to an hors d'oeuvres dish, instead of on to individual plates.

● Add serving spoons or tongs to each section to add to the fun.

● Invite your child to be the 'server'. She should say to each person, 'Would you like some…?', to which the person must reply, 'Yes, please' or 'No, thank you'. Encourage your child to use the spoons and the tongs to serve the food, after which the recipient should say, 'Thank you'.

● Alternatively, let each person serve themselves from the tray, deciding on their own amounts and the order in which they eat the various foods. This often encourages poor eaters, for example, to take several small portions of a certain kind of food. The element of 'choice' and the fun of using 'serving' cutlery, such as an ice-cream scoop to serve mashed potato, will help to keep your child enjoyably focused on the meal, decreasing the possibility of confrontation.

Taking it further

● Be brave and let your child pour everyone a cold drink from a plastic jug into plastic tumblers on a cloth-free table. She will soon become an expert!

LEARNING OPPORTUNITY
● To make a simple, fun 'penguin' as a 'reminder' to ask to leave the table when a meal has been eaten.

YOU WILL NEED
A kitchen-roll tube; scissors; white paper; black and orange felt-tipped pens; sticky tape.

STEPPING STONES
Talk alongside others, rather than with them. Use talk to gain attention and initiate exchanges. Use action rather than talk to demonstrate or explain to others.

 EARLY LEARNING GOAL
Communication, language and literacy: Interact with others, negotiating plans and activities and taking turns in conversation.

Polite Penguin says...

Sharing the game
● Cut the kitchen-roll tube to 12cm long.
● Invite your child to draw a face on the tube.
● Encourage your child to draw two wings on the paper, colour them black, cut them out and stick them to the sides of the tube with sticky tape.
● Then, challenge your child to draw the feet, colour them orange, cut them out and stick them to the bottom of the tube with sticky tape.

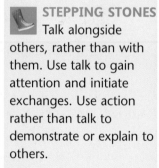

● When your child is eating his meal, ask him to keep 'Polite Penguin' under his chair until he has finished eating.
● Then, encourage your child to pick up Polite Penguin, put it on his fingers like a finger puppet, and say, 'Polite Penguin says, "Please, may I leave the table?"'.
● Polite Penguin can also be used as a reminder to your child to say 'please' and 'thank you' at other times.

Taking it further
● If your child is old enough, help him to write 'Please, may I leave the table?' on a piece of paper, by writing on top of your writing, copying underneath or trying to write and spell independently. Ask your child to draw a speech bubble around the words and to cut it out and attach it to Polite Penguin's face with sticky tape.

This chapter focuses on the outside world as encountered by young children on their journeys, perhaps to the childminder, nursery or school, to the shops, or even on a trip out. Children develop their knowledge and understanding of the world all the time, through first-hand experiences of what they see, hear, touch, smell and taste, as well as through the opportunity to talk about their discoveries with interested adults. Never underestimate the value of chatting with your child, even as you carry out the most mundane of chores! Sort out the washing into 'hot', 'medium' and 'cool' washes, and this will help your child to learn the vocabulary of colours and shades!

OUT AND ABOUT

THE WORLD AROUND THEM

The Knowledge and understanding of the world component of the Foundation Stage encompasses young children's learning about science, geography, design and information technology, and history. In scientific learning, the key experiences are exploration, through all of the five senses, of objects, events and living things, noticing similarities, differences, pattern and change, and discussion.

At the age of three, children enjoy matching real items with pictures, and making sets of the same items. By the age of four, they like to 'feel' with words, which are both accurate and expressive and that they can use themselves, such as 'mouldy' (of appearance) and 'precarious' (of balance). A five-year-

old child can usually make predictions or give reasons for things that they notice, such as what will happen to the hard, green tomato if it is left on the window sill, or why the slope of a disabled access ramp must not be too steep.

How you can help

● Invite your child to help you to collect and display lots of natural objects such as shells, stones, leaves and so on.
● Buy posters so that your child can make objects with the pictures, and play 'Odd one out' together, asking your child why one item is different from the rest.
● Make a 'feely box' (a carton covered in attractive, colourful wrapping paper with two holes cut in one side and an object inside) for your child to put his hands inside and feel an object to identify and describe.
● When you are out and about with your child, develop his geographical

understanding by getting to know the locality. Draw his attention to multicultural features such as places of worship, shops and so on.

● Take your child to see celebrations such as Chinese New Year processions.

● Talk about features of the environment that you both like, such as the park and its beautiful trees and flowers, and those that you dislike, such as litter.

DESIGN AND TECHNOLOGY

Design and technology skills are effectively developed by encouraging children to make 3-D models of places of interest visited, or to draw pictures. By the age of three, children can manage to build with chunky bricks, including food packaging, and as they grow, they can handle smaller and more intricate construction sets. Many five-year-olds like to draw pictures of the models that they make, as well as their own maps.

How you can help

● Store bricks and recyclable materials accessible to your child so that he can develop his planning skills, for example, 'I'll need this, then that, and maybe that…'.

● Adopt a problem-solving attitude, for example, if something does not work, say, 'Never mind! How else could we do this?'.

● Let your child try out a range of simple household tools and techniques such as a hole-punch, stapler and so on. Remember that children love to use 'in role' too, for example, using a hole-punch as the 'ticket collector' on the train.

● Giving your child a chance to experiment with different ways of joining things together is very important. Teach him the meaning of the word 'joiner' and let him pretend to be 'Jim the Joiner' (or 'Jane the Joiner' for a girl), under supervision where necessary!

INFORMATION TECHNOLOGY

Information technology is all around us. By the age of three, children can use programmable toys, while four-year-olds enjoy using tape recorders. At the age of five, children can, of course, be adept with CD-ROMS.

How you can help

● Draw your child's attention to electrical and technological devices both inside the home and outside.

● Give your child old telephones and radios to take apart and put together again.

● Always use the appropriate vocabulary when talking about technology such as 'rewind', 'fast forward',

'crash' and so on, which your child will readily absorb and relish using, for example, in his role-play.

A SENSE OF HISTORY

Children can show a sense of history as early as three years of age, for example, when they role-play their visit to the doctor's 'yesterday'. Old family photographs and articles such as old toys and household objects fascinate four- and five-year-olds.

How you can help

● Make up stories to tell your child about your family photographs.

● Use time language such as 'yesterday', 'today', 'before', 'afterwards', 'later', 'tomorrow', 'next', 'last', 'morning', 'afternoon', 'evening', 'soon', 'later' and so on.

● Devise some long-term growing projects with your child, such as growing herbs in pots.

LEARNING OPPORTUNITY
● To describe simple features of objects.

YOU WILL NEED
Fruit and vegetables (one item for your child and one for yourself) such as apples, bananas, oranges, potatoes, carrots and so on; drawstring bag; table.

STEPPING STONE
Examine objects and living things to find out more about them.

EARLY LEARNING GOAL
Knowledge and understanding of the world: Find out about, and identify, some features of living things, objects and events they observe.

That's mine!

Sharing the game

● Choose one kind of fruit or vegetable and place one for your child and one for yourself on the table.
● Say, 'Let's look really carefully at these apples' and help your child to describe what she sees. Talk about colour, shade, shape and size. Ask her to say whether any of the marks have interesting shapes that remind her of other things.
● Begin with using different varieties of, for example, apples that are fairly easy to tell apart. As your child gets used to looking carefully and talking about what she sees, use just one variety.

● Put the items in the drawstring bag and take one out each.
● Ask your child to look very carefully at her item, then to look for special things about it that she can remember.
● Let you child see you looking closely at your own item.
● Return both items to the bag.
● Open the bag and gently shake out the fruit or vegetables on to the table.
● Ask your child to find the item that she chose and to say how she knows that it is hers.
● Describe to her how you know you have found your own item.

Taking it further

● Use a plastic magnifying glass to look at the fruit or vegetables in more detail.
● Observe nature objects found on walks, such as leaves, stones, cones, conkers, acorns and shells.

LEARNING OPPORTUNITY
● To match a simple drawing of an outside feature with the 'real thing'.

YOU WILL NEED
Plain paper notepad; felt-tipped pens or pencil crayons; scissors.

 STEPPING STONE
Describe simple features of objects and events.

EARLY LEARNING GOAL
Knowledge and understanding of the world: Find out about, and identify, some features of living things, objects and events they observe.

Snap!

Sharing the game

● Before going on a short walk with your child, draw a simple outline picture of an easily identifiable object or environmental feature that you know you will be passing. Examples of drawings could be a post-box, a fairly distinctive

regularly parked vehicle, a pattern on the gable of a nearby house, architectural features on buildings such as places of worship, a distinctive gate, railings, door, garden feature, manhole cover and so on. Add some of the main colours to your drawing.
● Talk to your child about the picture before you go for your walk, including the design, purpose or any interesting facts about the feature.
● Give your child the picture to hold on your walk and ask him to say 'Snap!' when he sees the matching real thing.
● On another occasion, encourage your child to draw a picture of something for you to look for.
● Another time, make little booklets of drawings for each other with three or four pages stapled together.

Taking it further

● On an outing to the supermarket, give your child a label from one of the items that you will be buying that shows the name of the item.
● Read the name of the item with your child and talk about its place of origin, how it is grown, packaged, transported, cooked and so on.
● Ask your child to look for the item for you as you shop.

OUT AND ABOUT

OUT AND ABOUT

LEARNING OPPORTUNITY
● To remember a special 'spot' on a very short trail and to describe it.

YOU WILL NEED
Two children; two adults; very small ball of wool; scissors; stone; piece of card, approximately 10cm x 4cm.

STEPPING STONE Show an interest in the world in which they live.

EARLY LEARNING GOAL
Knowledge and understanding of the world: Find out about and identify features in the place they live and the natural world.

Follow that trail!

Sharing the game
● Ask an adult to amuse one of the children, out of sight of the second child and yourself.
● Give the second child the ball of wool and the stone. Ask her to walk slowly around a quiet outdoor area, such as a garden, and to unwind the wool as she walks.
● Invite her to choose a 'spot' to put the stone on top of the wool.

● Meet her at the end of the trail and help her to cut the wool.
● Tell the first child that the trail is now ready.
● Give him the card and ask her to pick up the 'start' of the wool.
● Help him to tie the wool around the card, knot it and wrap the wool over and over as he walks.
● Ask him to look for the stone, pick it up and try to remember where it was, by looking at what is near by.
● When he has finished the trail, ask him to say where he found the stone, for example, 'Next to the hole in the fence' or 'Near to the yellow rose bush'.
● On another occasion, add another stone, or hide a small 'treasure' at the end of the trail.

Taking it further
● Draw a simple map of your local environment, showing 'hidden treasure' very close to where you live.
● Hide a small 'treasure' near by, such as in a privet hedge, for your child to find using the map.

LEARNING OPPORTUNITY
● To make a book of 'shop windows'.

YOU WILL NEED
Sheets of plain paper, approximately A3 size; notepad of plain paper; stapler; felt-tipped pens; ruler; shopping catalogues or magazines; glue (optional); scissors.

 STEPPING STONE
Comment and ask questions about where they live and the natural world.

EARLY LEARNING GOAL
Knowledge and understanding of the world: Find out about and identify features in the place they live and the natural world.

Shop windows

Sharing the game
● On separate pieces of the notepad paper, write down the names of two or three shops or cafés that you pass regularly. (Use initial capital letters, then lower-case letters. Choose a variety of shops, if possible, such as a toy or pet shop, hardware store, optician's, multicultural clothes shops and eating places.
● Read the names of the places with your child and talk about what the shops sell, the kind of food served and so on.
● Taking the names with you, visit the shops and look carefully at the items in their windows or the features on their frontage.
● If possible, write the shop names again underneath your original names, copying the lettering that is on the shop fronts.
● At home, help your child to staple the large sheets of paper together to make a book, including a front and back cover.
● Ask your child to write 'Shop windows' on the front cover with a felt-tipped pen or, if necessary, write it in pencil for him and let him write over the top.

● On each page, rule a large rectangle to represent a shop window or frontage.
● Write the shop or business name above the window.
● Ask your child to draw some of the items or features that he saw in each 'window' space.

Taking it further
● Make a book of places of interest that you have visited and let your child draw appropriate pictures on each page.

All change!

Sharing the game
● On a shopping trip to the supermarket, ask your child to think of some items that would change in appearance or texture over a few days when brought home. Suggest the items in 'You will need' (see left).

● Once home, encourage your child to make simple drawings of the items that you have bought.
● Sprinkle the cress seeds on damp cotton wool in a yoghurt pot.
● Observe all the items together every few days and describe any changes.
● After about a week, compare the items with your child's drawings and talk about the changes.

Taking it further
● Ask your child some amusing questions, for example, 'Why would a cake get smaller?' or 'Why does the purse get lighter?'.
● Explain to your child that the world that we see around us can change in appearance, too.
● Buy postcards of your local area from a post office or newsagent's. (These are often highly flattering and taken from unusual angles!)
● Talk about how the postcard views might appear different from what you both see in reality.
● Talk about the reasons for this, for example, seasonal changes, the absence of traffic and litter, the angle at which the picture was taken and so on.
● Alternatively, take three photographs of your child, at the same outdoor spot, such as by the same tree, in summer, autumn and winter and talk about the changes.

LEARNING OPPORTUNITY
● To notice and re-create a miniature disabled access ramp.

YOU WILL NEED
Construction toys with wheels, such as Duplo or Sticklebricks; play bricks; small-world person; sticky tape; scissors; large brown carton; pictures of wheelchairs from newspapers or magazines, if possible.

 STEPPING STONE Talk about what is seen and what is happening.

EARLY LEARNING GOAL Knowledge and understanding of the world: Ask questions about why things happen and how things work.

Easy access

Sharing the game
● Talk to your child about people who use wheelchairs. If possible, look at pictures of wheelchairs in newspapers and magazines, and notice some wheelchair users when outside.
● Explain to your child that anyone who uses a wheelchair finds steps and kerbs difficult or impossible to use, and that is why it is important to have ramps.
● Say that people using walking sticks, crutches, baby buggies or shopping trolleys also appreciate ramps.
● When outside, point out ramps, lifts and platforms on certain buses and ambulances, fold-up ramps at train stations, ramps used for taxis and so on.

● At home, ask your child to make a wheelchair from Duplo or Sticklebricks, with a small-world person inside.
● Cut a piece of cardboard from the carton, approximately 40cm x 20cm, to create a ramp.
● Raise the ramp on play bricks at one end.
● Let your child discover himself that if the play bricks are too high, the ramp will be too steep and the wheelchair will move too quickly downwards, as well as being difficult to move upwards.

Taking it further
● Show your child a public toilet for disabled people and point out features such as very wide doors, low-height toilets and basins, grip handles and so on.
● Point out parking spaces for disabled drivers and ask your child why he thinks that they are close to buildings.

LEARNING OPPORTUNITY

● To construct models of local places such as a shopping centre, swimming-pool or garden centre.

YOU WILL NEED

Recyclable materials such as cereal packets or food and toiletries packaging; shopping carrier bags and catalogues; bubble wrap; old floral greetings cards; brown envelopes; small-world people, chairs and tables; play bricks; toy cars; scissors; sticky tape; glue; spreader; felt-tipped pens; long balloons; silver foil.

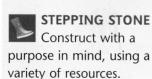

STEPPING STONE

Construct with a purpose in mind, using a variety of resources.

EARLY LEARNING GOAL

Knowledge and understanding of the world: Build and construct with a wide range of objects, selecting appropriate resources, and adapting their work where necessary.

I can build that

Sharing the game

● Cut open the cereal packets, flatten them, then reassemble them inside out and secure with sticky tape.

● When you are out and about, encourage your child to notice any special things that she can incorporate into a model, such as a disabled access ramp.

● At home, discuss with your child what she could use to make the model.

● Ideas could include:

Shopping centre – cut off the names of the shops on the carrier bags and stick them across the tops of the cereal packets. Draw products in the 'window' or use pictures cut from the catalogues. Make card ramps in front of the shops and use toy furniture for cafés. Put toy cars in the car park.

Swimming-pool – use bubble wrap.

Garden centre – cut out flowers from old greetings cards and stick them on to brown envelopes to make flower beds.

Optional features – use long balloons secured with sticky tape to make a bouncy castle. Make little balls from silver foil, enclosed by

play bricks, to create a ball pool.

Taking it further

● Cut around the edges of empty food packets so that they open, and stick pictures of appropriate products inside.

● ●

THINK FIRST!
Use this game to talk about why children must never use electrical and technological equipment by themselves and must never put their fingers near or in electrical sockets.

STEPPING STONE
Show an interest in ICT.

EARLY LEARNING GOAL
Knowledge and understanding of the world: Find out about and identify the uses of everyday technology and use information and communication technology and programmable toys to support their learning.

Technology all around!

Sharing the game
● Look around your home with your child and notice lights and electrical appliances. Talk about safety issues.
● Observe appliances that use batteries and tell your child that they are not toys.
● Explain to him that many things that use electricity can also be called technological.
● Tell your child that technological items often have a number display that gives us special information. Say that some are plugged in to electricity – for example, televisions, video recorders, CD players, radio-alarm clocks, computers, washing machines and refrigerators and some items, such as watches and mobile phones, use a battery.
● Go on a walk with your child and find out how many technological things you can see outside, such as telephones, bar-code scanners, revolving billboards, traffic-lights and so on.

Taking it further
● Challenge your child to make replicas of electrical and technological devices from recyclable materials, to use in role-play.
● Ideas could include:
Hairdryer or power drill – paper cup stuck on to a toothpaste box with string for the flex and card for the plug.
Computer monitor – cardboard box with paper screen.
Computer keyboard – cut open a large tissue box, flatten it, then reassemble it, inside out and upturned, and secure with sticky tape. Attach white sticky labels with numbers and letters written on.

How can we make that?

Sharing the game
● When out and about with your child, look out for interesting events that she will find fascinating. She will learn a great deal through chatting with you about them.
● Set out a few appropriate resources and encourage your child to try to work out what to do with them herself, rather than showing her straight away.
● Ideas could include:
Demolition vehicle – silver-foil ball attached to string with sticky tape and threaded through two holes in a toothpaste box, with a split-pin fastener at the bottom for the winder. Attach it to construction toy wheels with sticky tape.

Car 'on tow' – small cardboard squares with a hole punched in them, attached with sticky tape to the front and back ends of cars. Use a treasury tag as the tow rope slotted through the holes.

Taking it further
● Say the rhyme 'Chimney Pot' (see page 127) with your child.
● Go on an indoor 'How is it joined?' hunt, looking at doors to door frames, bolts to doors, light sockets to walls, fabric to chair bottoms and so on.

LEARNING OPPORTUNITY
● To notice differences in their appearance in the past and the present.

YOU WILL NEED
Photographs of your child taken in the past; mirror.

STEPPING STONE
Begin to differentiate between past and present.

EARLY LEARNING GOAL
Knowledge and understanding of the world: Find out about past and present events in their own lives, and in those of their families and other people they know.

Then and now

Sharing the game
● Show your child photographs of himself taken in the past, for example, in the garden, at the park, on the beach or indoors.

● Let him look in the mirror and talk about the differences in his appearance between 'then' and 'now', for example, 'My hair is shorter now'.
● Encourage him to talk about any of the objects or clothes in the photographs, for example, 'We gave that baby walker to baby Josh when I didn't need it any more' or 'I can't wear those swimming trunks any more because they're too small for me now'.

Taking it further
● Give your child different photographs of himself such as at age one, two and three, and encourage him to put them in age order.
● Show your child photographs of yourself and other family members at the age that your child is now. Talk about similarities and differences such as in appearance, clothes and objects.
● Put a current family photograph, your child's drawings and some small items inside a plastic box and keep it as a 'time capsule'!
● Decide together where to hide the 'capsule' in the house, such as in the loft, or where to bury it in the garden.
● Explain how exciting it will be to open the capsule in the future, when your child is older.
● Buy, or borrow from the library, a local history book of old photographs of your area showing your local shops, and talk about the differences.

LEARNING OPPORTUNITY
● To differentiate between morning and afternoon activities.

YOU WILL NEED
Two sheets of plain A4 paper; felt-tipped pens; scissors; drawstring bag.

STEPPING STONE
Begin to differentiate between past and present.

EARLY LEARNING GOAL
Knowledge and understanding of the world: Find out about past and present events in their own lives, and in those of their families and other people they know.

Morning or afternoon?

Sharing the game
● When going out in the morning with your child, draw her attention to features that she can associate with morning time, such as postpeople, milk and newspaper delivery people, and school children crossing the road towards school with a crossing patrol attendant.
● On afternoon outings, talk about features that tell you it is afternoon, for example, an ice-cream van parked outside the school gates or school children walking away from school.
● Fold a piece of paper into six sections. Draw three morning pictures and three afternoon pictures and cut them out. Include a back view of your child on the morning picture as she goes into nursery or school, and a front view on the afternoon picture as she leaves for home.
● Cut a section from the second sheet of paper and write 'Miss a turn' on it.
● Talk with your child about whether the pictures are morning or afternoon.
● Put the pictures and the 'Miss a turn' piece of paper into the bag.
● Invite your child to decide whether to collect the morning or afternoon pictures.

● Take turns to pick a piece of paper from the bag. If the incorrect picture is picked, it must be returned to the bag and the next player has their turn.
● The first person to collect their set of three chosen pictures is the winner.

Taking it further
● Ask your child to draw three 'morning' and 'afternoon' pictures of something that she does indoors, for example, brush her teeth.

LEARNING OBJECTIVE
● To describe how they feel at parades, special events such as celebrations and religious street carnivals, fairs, the circus and so on.

YOU WILL NEED
Two sheets of plain A4 card; felt-tipped pens; scissors; split-pin fastener.

 STEPPING STONE
Gain an awareness of the cultures and beliefs of others.

EARLY LEARNING GOAL
Knowledge and understanding of the world: Begin to know about their own cultures and beliefs and those of other people.

I felt so...

Sharing the game
● Cut a strip off the bottom of one sheet of card, approximately 3cm deep, and draw a red smiling mouth on it.
● Draw a face without a mouth on one side of the rest of the sheet of card.
● Attach the smiling mouth with the split-pin fastener so that it can be moved to make a happy face or a sad face.

● On the other side of the card, draw a surprised face.
● On one side of the second sheet of card, draw a cross face.
● On the other side, draw a slightly scared or nervous face.
● Talk to your child about what happened at a special occasion and about how he felt at certain key moments.
● Encourage your child by telling him how you felt, not only on the occasion in question, but also, perhaps, on a memorable occasion from your childhood, for example, how you felt nervous the first time you visited Father Christmas in his grotto, or saw a Chinese dragon.
● Let your child use the feelings cards as he talks.

Taking it further
● Cut out pictures from magazines of people's faces showing different expressions. Talk about how they look, and speculate on what they might be thinking.
● Turn the sound down on television programmes, particularly soap operas, and chat with your child about what the characters might be feeling, thinking or saying.

CHAPTER 5

LET'S PRETEND

All children are creative and make connections between one Area of Learning and another. Creative development includes art, music, dance, and role-play and imaginary play.

Children need to explore and experiment with natural and man-made media, materials, tools and sensations through body movements and all their senses. Try to provide a wide range of experiences, always 'feeding in' the correct vocabulary. As children begin to discover, for example, how paint and clay behave, or how the sounds of percussion instruments can be changed, they begin to represent what they see and feel about their world through drawing, painting, making models, music, dancing and 'make-believe' play.

DRAWING

At the age of three, children's scribble-drawing is a very important way through which they develop an understanding of spatial concepts. For example, vertical, horizontal and circular scribbles indicate that children are exploring the concepts of 'up and down', 'there and back' and 'round and round'. Between the ages of approximately three and a half and four, some children begin to deliberately draw lines around a space, then give the resulting shape a name as they start to use drawing to represent things, for example, a car, a tree or a house. At this stage, some children start to show an interest in colouring inside their drawings. By the age of five, children can draw detailed pictures, with background features.

How you can help
● Look out for any repeated movements or interests that your child seems to be concentrating on over a period of time, for example, twirling round and round when running outside, spinning objects around, or wrapping things up and putting them inside others, such as bags, envelopes and so on.
● Try to 'tune in' to your child's learning wavelength by providing related experiences, books, appropriate vocabulary and drawing opportunities to develop her interest. For example, give her circular pieces of paper and finger-paints to paint snail-shell circles or spirals.

● Think large and let your child experience drawing using large body movements. For example, put a long piece of wallpaper (facing downwards) on to a washable floor and invite your child to dip a small plastic car into a polystyrene container of ready-mixed paint, then let her crawl along the paper and make car tracks.

PAINTING

Three-year-olds enjoy experimenting with different-coloured blobs of paint, and then go on to explore one main colour at a time. They consciously start to arrange rough patterns of colour such as stripes or dots and usually name their pictures afterwards. At approximately four years old, children are very keen to experiment with mixing colours. They can also often say beforehand what they are going to paint. By the

age of five, children are painting representational pictures and also show an interest in combining different media such as sticking collage items on top of a painting to give a three-dimensional effect.

How you can help
● If possible, vary your child's types of paint, for example, ready-mixed, palette or powder.
● Provide different-sized paintbrushes and paper in different colours, shapes, sizes and textures.
● Teach your child the correct names for colours, for example, indigo and violet, and the correct names for shades, for example, light brown and dark blue.

MODEL-MAKING
By the age of three, children are experimenting with building towers of bricks and empty food cartons, often for the sheer fun of knocking them down. At three and a half,

children are interested in using bricks for walls, farms, zoos and houses. They are keen on box modelling and learning the best ways of joining boxes together. Between the ages of three and four, children are finding out about the different properties of play dough, Plasticine and clay, and at four years plus, they can begin to model according to their own intentions.

How you can help
● Provide the 'raw materials' and let your child experiment.
● Do not expect a finished product every time – the value is in the 'doing' as much as the result.
● Say to your child, 'Tell me about your model' or 'How did you make that?', rather than 'What is it?'.

MUSIC AND DANCE
At the age of three, children very much enjoy joining in with singing and dancing games, with adult support. They are experimenting with the sounds of ready-made and home-made percussion instruments, and can match these by their sounds. By the age of four, children can sing some songs on their own, and enjoy adapting familiar ones and making up their own. They can clap simple rhythms, such as their names, and enjoy finding out how sounds can be changed. At four years plus, children can sing many songs on their own, experiment with tuned instruments and, because they can respond to different moods in music, such as happy, sad and so on, they can start to express themselves through music, for example, by thinking of appropriate sound effects for stories, rhymes and poems.

How you can help
● When you are singing together, make up your own actions and copy each other.
● Play games in which body movements match sounds, for example, stamping to loud music, stretching upwards to 'high' music and so on.
● Have fun making up rhythm or sound-pattern games for each other to copy, for example, 'Clap twice, stamp twice, clap twice'.
● Whenever possible, let your child experiment with real instruments to find out whether they are blown, beaten, plucked or bowed.

ROLE-PLAY AND IMAGINARY PLAY
Three-year-olds delight in role-play and imitating everyday actions such as driving and cooking. They usually add their own sound effects and they begin to use an object to represent something else if they are similar in appearance – for example, a plastic plate for a steering wheel. By the age of four, role-play can be more imaginary, for example, being astronauts and magic characters, and props can be less obviously representational, for example, small bricks as food. Children now use words to represent an imaginary situation. At the age of five, children can devise elaborate fantasy play, often in groups, involving a narrative action and talking in dialogue to one another.

How you can help
● Play lots of games with your child involving miming, such as 'Here We Go Round the Mulberry Bush'.
● Devise your own games based on family events. Let your child improvise as much as possible using recyclable materials, for example, lengths of fabric, cartons and cushions. This develops creativity and problem-solving skills.

LEARNING OPPORTUNITY
● To experiment with mixing paint colours.

YOU WILL NEED
A plastic transparent tumbler; water; yellow, red and blue food colouring; yellow, red and blue ready-mixed paints; teaspoon; straws; yoghurt pots; paintbrushes; tissues.

STEPPING STONE Explore what happens when they mix colours.

EARLY LEARNING GOAL
Creative development: Explore colour, texture, shape, form and space in two or three dimensions.

Colour wizards!

Sharing the game
● Half-fill the tumbler with water.
● Put three drops of yellow food colouring on to the teaspoon and ask your child to mix it into the water.
● Invite your child to predict what colour the water will turn if she adds three drops of red colouring to the water.
● Put three drops of red colouring on to the teaspoon and ask your child to drop it into the tumbler.

● Let your child 'swizzle' the colours around with a straw (her 'colour wizard's magic swizzle stick') and watch the water change to orange.
● Encourage your child to say whether she thinks that this really is 'magic' or 'science'.
● Throw away the water and half-fill the tumbler again.
● Repeat the experiment with three drops of red colouring and three drops of blue colouring to make purple, then using three drops of blue colouring and three drops of yellow colouring to make green.
● Ask your child to do the same experiments with ready-mixed paint using the yoghurt pots for mixing.
● Encourage your child to predict each time what the 'new' colour will be.

Taking it further
● Let your child experiment with adding a small amount of black paint to ready-mixed paints to make dark shades, and white paint to make light shades.
● Ask your child to try matching felt-tipped pens to colours and shades on paint charts (available from DIY shops).

LEARNING OPPORTUNITY

● To create and paint a rainbow.

YOU WILL NEED

A plastic transparent tumbler; two sheets of white A4 paper; pencil; ready-mixed red, yellow, blue, black and white paints; paintbrush; yoghurt pots.

 **STEPPING STONE**
Begin to differentiate colours.

 EARLY LEARNING GOAL
Creative development: Explore colour, texture, shape, form and space in two or three dimensions.

Rainbow magic

Sharing the game

● On a very sunny day, put a sheet of paper on a window sill.

● Fill the tumbler with water and stand it on the paper.

● Move the tumbler carefully so that a bright shaft of sunlight catches the water and creates a strongly coloured rainbow effect on the paper.

● By holding the glass higher against the window, it is often possible to enlarge the size of the 'rainbow'.

● Teach your child this song, to the tune of 'Yankee Doodle' (Traditional):
    Red and orange and yellow and green
    Blue, indigo and violet, too
    I know the colours in a rainbow
    Do you know them, too?

● Tell your child that indigo is dark purple, and that violet is light purple, then let him experiment with the paints.

● Draw eight feint curved lines on to the second sheet of paper and write the colours of the rainbow in between the lines.

● Ask your child to sing the song as she paints the bands of the rainbow, starting at the top with red.

● Let your child experiment with mixing the paints to create orange, green, indigo and violet (red and yellow = orange; blue and yellow = green; red, blue and a small amount of black = indigo; indigo and white = violet).

Taking it further

● Invite your child to paint a giant rainbow on the back of a piece of old wallpaper.

● ◐ ● ◐ ● ◐ ● ◐ ● ◐ ● ◐ ● ◐ ● ◐ ● ◐ ● ◐ ● ◐ ● ◐ ● ◐ ● ◐ ● ◐

LEARNING OPPORTUNITY
● To talk about how different things feel.

YOU WILL NEED
A tray; selection of non-plastic items (see 'Sharing the game', right); table; sheet; torch.

STEPPING STONE Use their bodies to explore texture and space.

EARLY LEARNING GOAL
Creative development: Explore colour, texture, shape, form and space in two or three dimensions.

In a dark, dark cave

Sharing the game
● Put approximately ten non-plastic items with various textures on a tray. Ideas could include: natural items such as shells, stones, leaves, bark, gourds and clay; food items such as a pepper, cauliflower, onion skins, rubbery cabbage leaf, pineapple, avocado pear, orange, coconut, pulses, pasta, breakfast cereals and jelly cubes; fabrics such as silk, velvet, corduroy, lace and angora, and household items such as soap, brushes, pan scourer and bunch of keys.
● Cover the table with the sheet.
● Tell your child that you are going to find out how different things feel using your hands, arms, legs, feet and faces!
● Ask your child to take off her socks and shoes and wear short sleeves. Do the same yourself.
● Turn off any lights, then sit together in the 'cave' under the table with the tray of items and take turns to choose one of them with the torch.
● Ask your child to close her eyes.
● Say, for example, 'This is a stone and it feels hard'.
● Stroke your child's arm, hand, leg, foot or face with the item.
● Swap roles so that your child chooses an item for you to feel.
● Together, find words to describe the textures, for example, 'rough', 'smooth', 'hard', 'soft', 'cool', 'slimy', 'sticky', 'prickly', 'bumpy', 'crumbly' and so on.

Taking it further
● Make a 'feely box' from a large carton covered with colourful wrapping paper, with two holes cut in one side.
● Place an item inside and ask your child to put her hands in the box, describe what the item feels like and guess what it is.

Fun with five

Sharing the game
● Tell your child that we have five senses – sight, hearing, smell, touch and taste.
● On separate occasions, play some of the following sensory games:
Looking – Wrap some objects with tin foil for your child to guess what they are.
Listening – Collect six small identical food packets, put rice in two of them, pasta in two and coins in two, then secure them with sticky tape. Ask your child to shake the packets and match the 'pairs'.

Smelling – Draw and colour a fruit or flower. Put a drop of shampoo on to the picture, in a matching fragrance if possible, or lightly rub some scented soap on top, then invite your child to smell the picture.
Touching – Ask your child to identify items under soapy water.
Tasting – Take turns to concoct 'fruit cocktails' using cartons of different-flavoured fruit juices. Mix a tablespoon of one juice with a tablespoon of another juice, then challenge each other to identify the two flavours.

Taking it further
● Make up a 'sense riddle' based on two or three senses, for example, 'It looks like an umbrella, it feels like skin, it smells like soil. What is it? A mushroom!'.

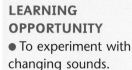

LET'S PRETEND

LEARNING OPPORTUNITY
● To experiment with changing sounds.

YOU WILL NEED
Bought or home-made percussion instruments, for example, bells, tambourine, drum, home-made shaker (pasta shells in a yoghurt pot covered with paper and sticky tape) and so on; two straws; tin foil; sticky tape.

STEPPING STONE
Explore and learn how sounds can be changed.

⭐ EARLY LEARNING GOAL
Creative development: Recognise and explore how sounds can be changed, sing simple songs from memory, recognise repeated sounds and sound patterns and match movements to music.

Conductor fun

Sharing the game
● Together, experiment with the instruments to see how many different kinds of sounds can be made with each one, according to how it is held or moved. A shaker will sound different depending upon whether it is shaken or rolled across the floor; a tambourine can be shaken quickly, slowly, loudly or quietly; the bells can be tapped with the fingers, and the 'skin' of the drum can be drummed with the fingers, or the fingers can rotate around the top of the skin to create a 'swishing' sound.

● As your child makes different sounds, talk about what she is doing, for example, 'Now you are playing quicker and louder!'.
● Make a baton by joining the straws end to end and covering them with tin foil.
● Show your child how to use the baton to be an orchestra conductor. Take turns to conduct each other in playing quicker, slower' and so on.
● Recite nursery rhymes quickly, slowly, loudly and quietly.

Taking it further
● Speak or sing in high or low voices, stretching arms up high and bending down low towards the floor.
● Show your child how to hold the baton horizontally and move it upwards, saying 'high' in a high voice, as you stretch up high.
● Make up simple dance stories, for example, 'The baby elephant was sad and lonely. Then his friends came and they all danced a funny wild dance!'.

That's me!

Sharing the game

● Share some rhyme books with your child and have fun, substituting his name, for example, 'Diddle, diddle, dumpling, My son Josh, Went to bed with his trousers on!'.

● Find some rhymes mentioning animals and substitute the names of other animals, for example, 'Hickory dickory dock, The monkey ran up the clock!'.

● Choose rhymes in which you can substitute your child's name and other details, for example, 'Josh had a little tiger, It loved to play in the snow. And everywhere that Josh went, The tiger was sure to go!'.

● Photocopy a photograph of your child's face, cut it out and ask him to draw the rest of his body as he walks to the shop being followed by the tiger!

Taking it further

● Make three more photocopies of your child's face.

● Ask your child to draw in details showing him 'featuring' in different rhymes.

● Write out each rhyme in clear lower-case lettering on separate sheets of paper, with a new title for each one, for example, 'Josh had a little tiger' and so on.

● Staple the sheets together to make a personalised rhyme book.

● Ask your child to put his forefinger on top of yours, and read the rhymes out loud together as you point to each word.

● Encourage your child to try to read the rhymes by himself, pointing to the words one at a time.

LET'S PRETEND

LEARNING OPPORTUNITY
● To role-play a real-life experience, then develop it imaginatively.

YOU WILL NEED
Four small toys; four small food cartons; four sheets of used Christmas wrapping paper; sticky tape (on dispenser, if possible); string or wool; scissors; old Christmas card; hole-punch; felt-tipped pens; red crêpe paper; cotton wool; tray; pillowcase.

STEPPING STONE
Engage in imaginative and role-play based on own first-hand experiences.

EARLY LEARNING GOAL
Creative development: Use their imagination in art and design, music, dance, imaginative and role-play and stories.

Santa's little helpers

Sharing the game
● Talk to your child about what is involved when wrapping presents, for example, using the correct amount of paper, folding it, using a sticky-tape dispenser or tying a knot, and so on.
● Invite your child to be one of Santa's little helpers and wrap some Christmas toys.
● Let your child wear a Santa hat (red crêpe paper decorated with cotton wool).
● Ask your child to put four toys inside four small food cartons and secure the flaps with sticky tape.
● Help your child to estimate how much of a sheet of paper she will need to wrap the present, and help her cut to it.
● Encourage your child to wrap each box in paper and secure it with sticky tape.

● Help your child to cut a piece of string or wool and tie it around the presents for extra strength.
● Encourage your child to cut out four labels from the Christmas card and punch a hole in each.
● Help your child to write a child's name on each label and tie one to each present.
● Invite your child to put the presents in the sack (pillowcase) and the sack on to Santa's sleigh (tray) 'ready for the journey'.

Taking it further
● Make up the rest of the story together. Write it down and read it again at bedtime.

LEARNING OPPORTUNITY
● To bring a photograph 'to life'.

YOU WILL NEED
A photograph of your child with other children; Blu-Tack; cereal box; scissors; sticky tape; small-world people, animals, furniture and so on; play dough; paper; card; felt-tipped pens; tray.

STEPPING STONE
Describe experiences and past actions, using a widening range of materials.

EARLY LEARNING GOAL
Creative development: Express and communicate their ideas, thoughts and feelings by using a widening range of materials, suitable tools, imaginative and role-play, movement, designing and making, and a variety of songs and musical instruments.

Guess what happened!

Sharing the game
● Together, choose an 'active' photograph of your child with other children, for example, at a birthday party.
● Cut open the cereal box and stick the photograph on to one side with Blu-Tack.
● Cut out two 'hinges' from the remaining cereal box and attach them to the back of the photograph, so that it stands up.
● Together, talk about the events in the photograph.
● Stand the photograph on the tray and ask your child to suggest small-world items to make a scene of what happened, for example, people, furniture, play dough for food and so on.
● Together, draw and cut out any items that cannot be easily made, for example, draw party balloons along one edge of a piece of card attached with sticky tape at a right angle to the tray to represent a wall.
● Let your child re-enact the event in the photographs using the small-world toys.
● Prompt your child gently to introduce a fantasy element, for example, a magic elephant suddenly arriving at the party!

Taking it further
● Clear a shelf on a bookcase and attach a photograph with Blu-Tack at a right angle.
● Encourage your child to re-create the photograph's events with small-world items along the shelf and other hand-drawn 'background' pictures.

LEARNING OPPORTUNITY
● To improvise props for fantasy play and role-play.

YOU WILL NEED
Children's story-books; recyclable materials; household objects; small lengths of fabric; paper; felt-tipped pens; sticky tape.

STEPPING STONE
Use available resources to create props to support role-play.

EARLY LEARNING GOAL
Creative development: Use their imagination in art and design, music, dance, imaginative and role-play and stories.

What shall we use?

Sharing the game
● Look through some well-loved story-books with your child.
● Invite her to show you her favourite picture and to tell you about it. Ask, 'What happened next?'.
● Say, 'Let's pretend to be…' and 'Now what shall we use for…?'.
● Brainstorm ideas for props, using packaging such as cardboard boxes for buildings, vehicles and beds; cut-up egg-box sections for all kinds of food; general

household items such as cushions and old curtains for tents and dens, small lengths of fabric for capes, hoods and bridal trains, and so on.
● If something special is required, simply draw it together on a piece of paper or card, cut it out and attach it where it is needed with sticky tape, for example, a pumpkin for Cinderella, or a high-tech dashboard for a space rocket stuck to the back of a chair, with an astronaut wearing a helmet made from a plastic colander covered in tin foil.
● Occasionally, gently prompt your child by leaving a few component parts where she can see them, for an improvised creation. Leave her to make the connection and put the items together with perhaps a little help from you, for example, a mop head and tin-foil tube to represent a ride-on horse.

Taking it further
● Put small miscellaneous household items in a pillowcase.
● Take turns with your child to pick one out.
● Think up lots of 'pretend' ways of using it.

● ●

YOU WILL NEED
Children's television-based magazines; scissors; card such as backs of old greetings cards; glue; lollipop sticks or straws; sticky tape.

 STEPPING STONE
Begin to use talk instead of action to rehearse, reorder, and reflect on past experience, linking significant events from own experience and from stories, paying particular attention to sequence and how events lead into one another.

★ **EARLY LEARNING GOAL**
Communication, language and literacy:
Use language to imagine and re-create roles and experiences.

Favourite characters

Sharing the game

● Together, cut out pictures of your child's favourite television and video characters.
● Stick them on to the backs of old greetings cards, then cut around the card.
● Attach each picture to a lollipop stick or straw with sticky tape.
● Talk about an episode of one of your child's favourite programmes or videos.
● Encourage your child to retell the events of part or all of it.
● Give your child the stick puppet(s) and challenge him to 'talk' through them and to 'act out' the events. Encourage him to change or develop anything if he wishes.
● Another time, invite him to use the puppet(s) in a different setting so that he can create a new story from his imagination.

Taking it further

● Make a photocopy of a full-length photograph of your child.
● Cut around the photograph and stick it on to the back of an old greetings card.
● Cut around the card and stick it on to a lollipop stick to make a stick puppet of your child.

● Let your child use his puppet together with his television puppet(s) to help him to link events in his own life with what he has seen on the television or video.
● Display your child's puppets in upturned papier-mâché egg-boxes, with a slit cut in the bottom of each compartment.
● Push each puppet through a slot.

LEARNING OPPORTUNITY
● To retell an exciting event using shadow puppets.

YOU WILL NEED
Old greetings cards; felt-tipped pens; scissors; straws; sticky tape; white sheet; three chairs; table; table lamp.

STEPPING STONE
Try to capture experiences and responses with music, dance, paint and other materials or words.

EARLY LEARNING GOAL
Creative development: Express and communicate their ideas, thoughts and feelings by using a widening range of materials, suitable tools, imaginative and role-play, movement, designing and making, and a variety of songs and musical instruments.

Shadow puppets

Sharing the game

● Ask your child about an exciting event that she could recapture using shadow puppets, such as a holiday or visit to the zoo.
● Together, draw the simple outlines of family members, a car, aeroplane, distinctive animals and so on, on the greetings cards and cut them out.

● Wrap three straws together with sticky tape and stick them at a right angle to the bottom of each figure.
● Put the puppets on the table.
● Tuck two chairs underneath the table, with a space in between.
● Attach the white sheet between the chairs using sticky tape and make it as taut as possible.
● Place the table lamp on another chair behind the screen.
● Switch on the lamp and darken the room.
● Ask your child to stand behind one of the chairs and to hold the puppet flat against the sheet, where it will appear as a shadow.
● Encourage your child to tell the 'audience' what happened, for example, on holiday, using the puppets.

Taking it further
● Invite your child to tell an imaginary story using the puppets.
● Ask a second child to provide sound effects using percussion instruments or an electronic keyboard.
● Encourage another child to stand behind the other chair holding some puppets, so that there are two puppeteers.

LET'S PRETEND

LEARNING OPPORTUNITY
● To talk about preferences in pictures of flowers.

YOU WILL NEED
A cut flower from a supermarket or flower shop; two pictures (not photographs) representing it, for example, from old greetings cards, postcards, art books, calendars and so on.

 STEPPING STONE
Make comparisons.

 EARLY LEARNING GOAL
Creative development: Respond in a variety of ways to what they see, hear, smell, touch and feel.

Flowers all around

Sharing the game
● Find two different pictures of the same kind of flower and buy a bunch of the flowers.
● Show your child the flower and talk about how it looks, smells and feels.
● Discuss what you can see in the pictures and compare them with the real flower.
● Explain to your child that the pictures are not photographs and are not meant to look exactly the same as the real flower.

● Discuss what the artists have used to produce their pictures.
● Talk with your child about whether the pictures remind you both of anything, or make you think about something special, and how they make you feel.
● Ask your child which picture he likes the most, or prefers, and encourage him to say why.
● Tell your child which one you prefer and why.
● Explain how all artists work hard on their pictures and that this makes them happy. Say that they always know that some people will prefer other artists' pictures.

Taking it further
● Talk with your child about pictures in story-books, especially how they make you feel.
● Compare the pictures in two different versions of the same story, for example, a fairy-tale or traditional story.
● Ask your child to say which pictures he prefers and encourage him to say why.

CHAPTER 6

QUIET TIMES

Tom, aged five, is very worried that his baby brother, Adam, will knock down the carefully constructed pirate ship that he has built in his bedroom. He writes a notice – 'kip ut' – and sticks it on his bedroom door. His family understand what Tom is saying. So, Adam is allowed to look at the ship under supervision, the ship remains intact and Tom has learned the power of the written word!
This chapter focuses on ideas for quiet times at home, involving reading and writing, and new ways of using ready-made board games to develop mathematical understanding. There are also ideas for making pictures.

READING

Three-year-olds are beginning to 'read' the world, by realising that the signs and symbols that they see around them all carry a meaning, for example, trademarks on packaging and domestic appliances, traffic signs and advertisements, but also, of course, their names. By the age of four, children are beginning to work out the link between printed and spoken words, such as that, in English, we read from left to right, one word at a time, down the page. They show great interest in letters of the alphabet, especially in their names. They can play 'I spy' and link some letters with their sounds. At the age of five, children are recognising familiar words on sight and can start to 'sound out' regular two- and three-letter words, for example, 'zip'.

How you can help
● Whenever possible, point out 'environmental print' to your child.
● Draw one or two signs for your child to 'spot' on trips out.
● When playing 'Shop', cut out food labels to match packages that are being 'sold', and encourage your child to make a 'shopping list' to 'read' by sticking the labels with Blu-Tack on to a piece of card cut from a cereal packet.
● When reading with your child, put his forefinger on top of yours and point to each word in turn as you read out loud. Encourage your child to join in.
● On a sheet of paper, write out some well-known nursery rhymes and make small cards of certain words (or use sticky labels) for your child to match with the words on the sheet.
● Play lots of rhyme, rhythm and alliteration games involving physical action, to ensure that your child can distinguish one sound from another.

- Recite a nursery rhyme, leaving out a rhyming word for your child to supply, possibly physically, for example, 'Humpty Dumpty had a great...', 'Jack fell... and broke his crown' and so on.
- Play 'I spy', initially with two objects or pictures side by side, then three and so on.
- When your child is ready to 'sound out' words, use magnetic letters on a refrigerator door to make two- and three-letter words, and allow him ten seconds to read them.

WRITING

Three-year-olds love to engage in early 'pretend' or 'scribble' writing, which is distinct from drawing. Children do this for the sheer fun of covering a page and also as part of role-play, for example, a 'shopping list'. By the age of four, children's writing often contains letter-like attempts, possibly arranged in patterns. At the age of five, children

are able to use one letter to stand for a word, or even a group of words, and start to use invented spellings, attempting to represent all sounds. Four- to five-year-old children can be taught to write alphabet letters, starting with those in their names.

How you can help

- Let your child see you writing as much as possible. Explain what you are doing, including inputting text on a word processor, or a text message on a mobile phone.
- With your child, take part in lots of role-play situations involving writing, for example, taking orders in a café or take-away restaurant, writing appointments at the hairdresser's or writing doctors' prescriptions.
- When your child makes a model, encourage him to think of appropriate labels to write, such as the name of a ship or of a robot.
- Invite your child to explore the shape and direction of letters through whole body movements, for example, moving round and round, backwards and forwards and so on.
- Challenge your child to practise making circles and lines using large shoulder movements, for example, in the air or painting a fence with water.
- Help your child to practise pincer movements through crumbling bread crumbs, peeling sprouts, picking up small pieces of foil using tweezers and spring pegs, and so on.
- Encourage your child to practise how to hold a pencil correctly by developing finger

control through threading and finger-painting (see 'Hold it!' on page 87).
- Encourage your child to add small details to his drawings, for example, the pattern on a shirt.
- When practising writing alphabet letters, let your child write on top of your writing. Always start each letter at

the top and complete it in one flowing movement, as far as possible. When he is proficient at this, provide a 'starting dot' for each letter and let him copy your letters underneath.
- Write patterns, letters, words and sentences on sheets of A4 paper. Slip them inside a transparent plastic pocket, and ask your child to write on top of your marks with a felt-tipped pen, which can be wiped off each time.
- Use magnetic letters for spelling practice. Invite your child to be the teacher and encourage him to put together letters to make two- and three-letter words for you to read. Help him by sorting out five letters from which to choose.

LEARNING OPPORTUNITY
● To read the names of familiar shops.

YOU WILL NEED
Carrier bags from familiar shops visited by you and your child, for example, a supermarket, toyshops, children's clothes shop, 'baby' shop, bookshop and DIY store; items from each shop; table; chairs; old greetings cards; scissors; felt-tipped pens; string; CD or tape of lively music; CD player or tape recorder.

 THINK FIRST!
Never leave young children unsupervised with plastic bags.

 STEPPING STONE
Show interest in illustrations and print in books and print in the environment.

 EARLY LEARNING GOAL
Communication, language and literacy: Read a range of familiar and common words and simple sentences independently.

Musical bags

Sharing the game
● Cut the backs off the greetings cards.
● Write the name of each shop on the back of each card in lower-case lettering. If your child is unfamiliar with capital letters, use a lower-case letter at the beginning of each name.
● Place the items on the table.
● Attach a carrier bag to each chair, using string if necessary.
● Arrange the chairs as for 'Musical chairs'.
● Together, say the name of the shop on each bag. Talk about the kinds of items that are sold by each shop.
● Show your child one item at a time and ask her where she thinks it was bought.
● Play some music and invite your child to dance around the chairs.
● Stop the music and give your child an item. Ask her to put it in the correct bag and to say the name of the shop.
● When your child is familiar with recognising the names on the bags, remove them and replace them with the cards.
● Play the game as before.

Taking it further
● Put a tin of food or an empty packet on each chair.
● Write the names of the items on the backs of cards.
● When the music stops, ask your child to match a card with the correct item.

QUIET TIMES

LEARNING OPPORTUNITY
● To understand the one-to-one relationship between the spoken and the written word.

YOU WILL NEED
Nursery-rhyme book including 'Humpty Dumpty' (Traditional); old greetings card; felt-tipped pens; scissors; six wooden or plastic bricks; white A4 paper; sticky tape; white sticky labels.

STEPPING STONE
Understand the concept of a word.

EARLY LEARNING GOAL
Communication, language and literacy: Explore and experiment with sounds, words and texts.

Word bricks

Sharing the game
● Help your child to draw 'Humpty Dumpty' on the back of an old greetings card, then cut it out.
● Look at the nursery-rhyme book together and show your child the pictures of Humpty Dumpty and the words.
● Say to your child, 'Let's say the words out loud and point to them as we say them one at a time'.
● Encourage your child to put his forefinger on yours as you point to the words.
● Cut out six pieces of paper slightly smaller than the bricks, and write each of the words from 'Humpty Dumpty sat on a wall' on a piece.
● Attach each word to a brick with sticky tape. Say the first line of the rhyme together and, as you say each word, pick up the relevant brick and put it on the floor. Make Humpty 'fall off the wall'.

● Repeat the rhyme and ask your child to pick up a 'word brick' each time.
● Encourage your child to say the first line slowly again and put up a finger for each word.
● Ask your child to count his fingers, then the word bricks.

● Write the words on small white sticky labels and stick one on each of your child's fingers, starting with his left-hand thumb.
● Repeat the words and invite your child to lift up the appropriate finger each time.

Taking it further
● Replace the 'Humpty Dumpty' bricks with your child's first name and surname.

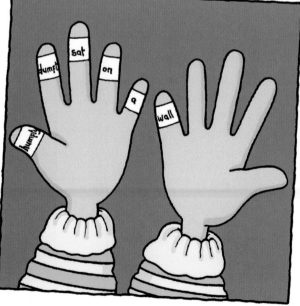

QUIET TIMES

LEARNING OPPORTUNITY
● To read familiar words.

YOU WILL NEED
Nursery-rhyme books and story-books; scissors; A4 paper; felt-tipped pens.

 STEPPING STONE
Begin to recognise some familiar words.

 EARLY LEARNING GOAL
Communication, language and literacy: Read a range of familiar and common words and simple sentences independently.

Read about me

Sharing the game
● Look through the books to find phrases or sentences that can be adapted to include your child's name, for example, 'Ruby Taylor had a farm and on that farm she had some cats' or 'Ruby climbed into the coach and went to the ball'. Choose sentences containing key words such as 'had', 'and', 'on', 'that', 'she', 'some', 'went' and so on.

● Turn a sheet of A4 paper horizontally and write one of the phrases or sentences above in large, lower-case letters.
● Write the words again on another piece of paper and cut them out.
● Ask your child to put the cut-up words on top of the words on the piece of paper. Give her just the key words while you match the remaining words, such as her name, or less usual words, for example, 'farm', 'coach' and so on.
● Remove the 'base' sheet of paper, then together, assemble the cut-up words so that they make sense. Place 'your' words first, then ask your child to put the key words in the correct places and read them as she does so.
● Make up and write sentences containing the same key words, for example, 'Ruby climbed into the rocket and went to the moon'.

Taking it further
● Practise 'sounding out' words by making 'rhyming booklets'.
● Write a word, for example, 'cat', and cut it out.
● Write and cut out alternative initial letters such as 'b', 'h', 'm' and 'r'.
● Staple the letters on top of the original initial letter so that different words can be read, for example, 'bat', 'hat', 'mat' and 'rat'.

 STEPPING STONE
Hear and say the initial sound in words and know which letters represent some of the sounds.

EARLY LEARNING GOAL
Communication, language and literacy: Link sounds to letters, naming and sounding the letters of the alphabet.

My name story

Sharing the game

● Write your child's name on the piece of notepaper.

● Make up a short fantasy story about your child, involving objects beginning with each letter in his name, for example, Owen – 'Owen was sitting on the beach when a big whale swam up to him, and then he saw an elephant with a necklace around its tail! The whale gave Owen a ride on its back and so did the elephant. Then the elephant gave Owen the necklace and Owen gave it to his mum!'.

● Write your child's name, spreading the letters out, with a felt-tipped pen on the first sheet of A4 paper.

● Draw an item that has the same initial sound above each letter.

● Place the sheet of paper into the wallet.

● On the second sheet of paper, write your child's name and cut out the letters.

● Tell your child the story, pointing to the objects that you have drawn.

● Emphasise the initial sounds of the objects and point out the letters underneath the pictures.

● Retell the story, pausing before saying the name of each object, and encourage your child to supply the missing words.

● Ask your child to place the matching cut-out letters on top of the letters on the first sheet of paper.

Taking it further

● Arrange the letters to spell your child's name.

● Invite your child to retell the story using the letters as 'cues'.

LEARNING OPPORTUNITY
● To learn to hold a pencil correctly.

YOU WILL NEED
Crumbly foods, for example, stock cube, dried herbs and pastry crumbs; glitter; small beads; bread; thick, preferably soft, pencil; paper.

THINK FIRST!
Never leave young children alone with very small items such as beads. Always supervise such activities.

STEPPING STONE
Begin to form recognisable letters.

EARLY LEARNING GOAL
Communication, language and literacy: Use a pencil and hold it effectively to form recognisable letters, most of which are correctly formed.

Hold it!

Sharing the game
● To develop the 'pincer' or 'tripod' grip necessary to hold a pencil between the thumb and forefinger, give your child lots of practice in crumbling food and sprinkling glitter using her thumb ('Tommy Thumb') and forefinger ('Peter Pointer').
● Give your child small beads to pick up one at a time.
● Break up a piece of bread into small pieces and invite your child to pick them up using her thumb and forefinger as a 'duck's beak'.
● Show your child the following 'pick and flick' technique for picking up a pencil, so that it is correctly positioned in her hand, without you having to reposition it for her each time:

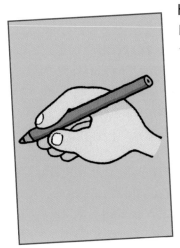

Right hand: place the pencil diagonally on the table, pick it up between the thumb and forefinger and 'flick' it backwards, using the middle finger ('Finger Tall'), so that the pencil is resting against the fingertip of the middle finger.
Left hand: reverse the pencil position on the table.
● If your child is left-handed, she will need to hold the pencil approximately 4cm from the point, so that she can see what he is writing and reduce 'smudging'. Her paper should be tilted slightly downwards and be to the left of her body.

Taking it further
● When your child can write fluently, use a timer to count how many times she can write her name in one minute.

 STEPPING STONE
Use writing as a means of recording and communicating.

EARLY LEARNING GOAL
Communication, language and literacy: Write their own names and other things such as labels and captions and begin to form simple sentences, sometimes using punctuation.

I can write my name!

Sharing the game
● Write your child's name in large, well-spaced lower-case letters on the piece of sandpaper with a black wax crayon.
● Add a red dot to each letter to show your child its 'starting-point'.

● On a sheet of paper, turned horizontally, write your child's name in pencil, adding the dots.
● Invite your child to 'stroke' the letters in his name on the sandpaper. Talk him through each letter, for example, 'Down, up to the top, round and finger off'.
● Ask your child to write his name in pencil on top of your pencilled letters.
● Underneath each letter, write approximately half of the letter, adding the dot.
● Encourage your child to complete each letter, starting at the dot.
● Challenge your child to try to write his name using only the starting dots.

Taking it further
● Once your child can write each letter correctly, help him to remember their order by writing the first two letters for him. Encourage him to trace on top of them with his finger.
● Invite your child to trace the letters 'in the air'.
● Cover the letters and ask your child to write them from memory.
● Using this technique, continue practising with your child, adding another letter each time.

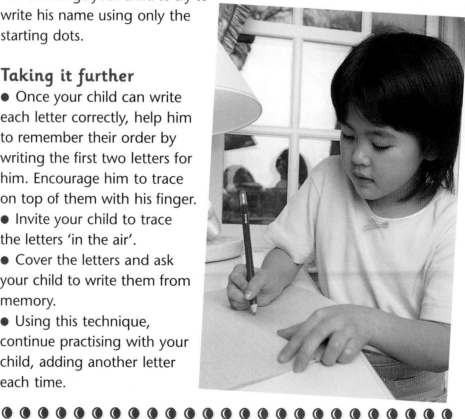

LEARNING OPPORTUNITY
● To incorporate 'pretend' writing into fantasy play.

YOU WILL NEED
A cardboard box, 30cm high; coloured plain paper; scissors; sticky tape; cling film; two examples of each of the following types of 'writing' (authentic, if possible, or handwritten replicas) – greetings cards, party invitation, postcard, letter, dental reminder card, prescription, shopping list, note for milk delivery person, telephone message, video label, gift tag and dressing-up clothes; simple props; pencil; writing pad.

STEPPING STONE
Use writing as a means of recording and communicating.

EARLY LEARNING GOAL
Communication, language and literacy: Attempt writing for different purposes, using features of different forms such as lists, stories and illustrations.

Fun writing box

Sharing the game
● Cover the cardboard box with coloured paper.
● Cut out one set of the different types of writing and attach them to the box with sticky tape.
● Cover the box with cling film.
● Put the second set of the different types of writing in the box.
● Over a period of time, talk to your child about the writing samples that are on the box and show her those that are inside.
● Ask your child to close her eyes, put her hand in the box and pick a sample.
● With your child, make up a short, amusing scenario involving the writing samples, which you can act out together. Ensure that your child has the role involving some 'pretend' writing.
● Provide your child with a pencil, paper, a few simple props and dressing-up clothes.
● Try to be as inventive as you can – for example, say, 'You send away for a toy elephant and a real one arrives!'.

Taking it further
● Whenever possible, arrange for your child to be involved in real writing situations that you have practised in your games. For example, use lower-case lettering for a note to the milk delivery person and let your child write on top of your writing or copy underneath.

Whose line?

Sharing the game

● Attach three small pieces of red paper and three small pieces of green paper on to the dice with sticky tape.

● Rule the sheets of white paper into one hundred squares, the same size as those on the gameboard.

● Write the numerals 1 to 100 on the squares, using the black felt-tipped pen, and cut them out.

LEARNING OPPORTUNITY
● To become familiar with number names and numerals beyond ten.

YOU WILL NEED
A 'Snakes and ladders' board; dice; small pieces of red and green paper; scissors; sticky tape; two sheets of A4 paper; ruler; pencil; black, red and green thin felt-tipped pens; coin.

● Together, arrange the numbers at the side of the table, line by line, as on the board, saying the numbers out loud.

● Toss the coin to decide who should go first.

● The first player should choose to be 'red' or 'green', then throw the dice.

● If the correct colour is thrown, the player should choose a line of paper numbers and use the appropriately coloured (red or green) felt-tipped pen to make a dot on each number as they say it out loud.

● The player should then put each number on top of the matching square on the board, saying it out loud again. The player has now 'won' the line.

● When all the lines on the board have been covered, the winner is the player with the most lines.

Taking it further

● Spread the numbered squares, face down, randomly on the table.

● Take turns to pick up a number, say it out loud and place it on the matching square on the board.

 STEPPING STONE
Begin to count beyond 10.

EARLY LEARNING GOAL
Mathematical development: Say and use number names in order in familiar contexts.

QUIET TIMES

LEARNING OPPORTUNITY
● To recognise numerals 1 to 6.

YOU WILL NEED
A 'Ludo' board; cling film; dice; six sultanas per person; two plastic plates; sheet of A4 paper; thin black felt-tipped pen; scissors; Blu-Tack.

💡 **THINK FIRST!**
Be aware of any food allergies or dietary requirements.

👢 **STEPPING STONE**
Recognise numerals 1 to 5, then 1 to 9.

⭐ **EARLY LEARNING GOAL**
Mathematical development: Recognise numerals 1 to 9.

Six sultanas

Sharing the game

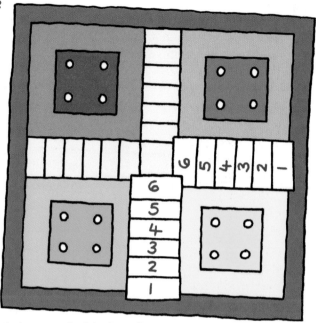

● Draw a 'ladder' for both of you, the same size as the 'square ladders' on the gameboard.
● Write the numerals 1 to 6 in each square and cut out the 'number ladders'.
● Invite your child to choose a colour from the board, and choose one for yourself.
● Place a 'number ladder' on each person's 'square ladder' and secure it with Blu-Tack.
● Invite your child to wash her hands with you.
● Cover the gameboard in transparent plastic film.
● Ask your child to help you to count out six sultanas on to each plate, saying, 'One for you, one for me'.
● Take turns to throw the dice. The first person to throw a 6 starts the game.
● When the person throws the dice, they should say the number thrown out loud, point to the matching numeral on their 'number ladder' and cover it with a sultana.
● If the number thrown has already been covered by a sultana, the person should wait for their next turn.
● If a 6 is thrown, the person has another turn.
● The winner is the first person to cover all six of their numbers, after which the sultanas may be eaten!

Taking it further
● Make 'number ladders' with the numerals 5, 6, 7, 8, 9, 10, cover the dice with white sticky labels numbered 5 to 10, and play the game.

LEARNING OPPORTUNITY
● To make a repeating pattern of two items.

YOU WILL NEED
A draughts set; coin; sheet of A4 paper.

STEPPING STONE Show an interest in shape and space by playing with shapes or making arrangements with objects.

EARLY LEARNING GOAL Mathematical development: Talk about, recognise and re-create simple patterns.

Draughts patterns

Sharing the game
● Mix the set of draughts pieces together and place them on the sheet of paper.
● Tell your child that 'his' line is the line of squares on the outer edge of the gameboard nearest to him and that 'your' line is the one nearest to you.
● Decide who will be 'heads' and who will be 'tails'.
● Toss the coin to decide who should go first.
● The first player should toss the coin and, if the toss is won, the first player can take a draughts piece from the sheet of paper and place it on a matching square of the line nearest to them, at the edge of the gameboard.

● If the toss is lost, the first player does nothing.
● Take turns to toss the coin.
● The winner is the first person to complete their line with four black and four white squares.
● The winner should touch the draughts pieces one at a time, starting at the left-hand side and say, 'Black, white, black, white, black, white, black, white. Have I won this game? Yes, that's right!'.

Taking it further
● Play the game, as above, placing the draughts pieces on a blank sheet of paper so that your child has to make the alternating sequence of black, white and so on for himself.
● Use a timer to see who can build the tallest tower of alternating black and white draughts pieces.

LEARNING OPPORTUNITY
● To watch colours flow into one another.

YOU WILL NEED
Bottles of red, blue, green and yellow food colouring; white A4 paper; six plastic dishes or yoghurt pots; thin and thick paintbrushes; tablespoon of icing sugar; tablespoon; water.

STEPPING STONE
Understand that different media can be combined.

EARLY LEARNING GOAL
Creative development: Explore colour, texture, shape, form and space in two or three dimensions.

Icing-sugar art

Sharing the game
● Pour a small amount from each bottle of food colouring into four separate dishes.
● Half-fill a dish with water (for rinsing paintbrushes).
● Together, put one level tablespoon of icing sugar into a dish.
● Add two tablespoons of cold water and mix.
● Invite your child to paint the mixture generously over a piece of paper, using the thick paintbrush.
● Encourage your child to use the thin paintbrush dipped in the food colourings (rinsed each time) to paint on the paper gently. The colours will 'run' and appear 'fuzzy'.
● Ask your child to flick her paintbrush and watch the drops of colouring 'splodge'.
● Help your child to tilt the paper gently from side to side to see the colours flowing into each other.
● Leave the painting to dry overnight into a very pretty, glazed 'marbled' effect.

Taking it further
● Encourage your child to mix the colours of the rainbow and paint a 'shimmering' rainbow. This looks most authentic, as if seen through a 'rain haze'.
● Invite your child to paint the sea using blue and dark-green paints, and to create a wave effect with his fingers.
● When the paper is dry, ask her to cut out multicoloured fish shapes, and to stick them on top of her 'sea' background.

LEARNING OPPORTUNITY
● To make a 'dressing doll' of themselves.

YOU WILL NEED
A photograph of your child's face; sheet of A4 paper; old greetings card; felt-tipped pen; scissors; three straws; sticky tape; four split-pin fasteners; children's clothes catalogues; Blu-Tack.

STEPPING STONE Make constructions, collages, paintings, drawings and dances.

EARLY LEARNING GOAL
Creative development: Explore colour, texture, shape, form and space in two or three dimensions.

How do I look?

Sharing the game
● Make a photocopy of a photograph of your child's face.
● Stick the copy of your child's face on to the blank side of an old greetings card.
● Give your child the card and ask him to draw a body, arms and legs

underneath his face. Then encourage him to cut out them out.
● Help your child to attach the arms and legs to the body with split-pin fasteners so that they can be moved.
● Together, wind sticky tape around three straws, then help your child to stick them with sticky tape to make a jointed 'stick puppet' of himself.
● Give your child a catalogue featuring children's clothes and help him to cut out clothes of his choice.
● Encourage your child to use a small amount of Blu-Tack to fix an outfit on to his stick puppet.
● Invite your child to 'talk through' a little scenario with his puppet.

Taking it further
● Photocopy the faces of other family members and let your child 'dress' them in the same way.
● Let your child draw in details or stick on collage materials to represent exciting clothes below the photocopy of his face, for example, a spacesuit, a uniform, a clown's outfit and so on.

LEARNING OPPORTUNITY
● To create 'aeroplane trails' in paint.

YOU WILL NEED
An old soft toothbrush; lollipop stick; sticky-tape dispenser; blue paper; white paint; saucer.

STEPPING STONE
Pretend that one object represents another, especially when objects have characteristics in common.

★ EARLY LEARNING GOAL
Creative development: Use their imagination in art and design, music, dance, imaginative and role-play and stories.

Flying toothbrushes

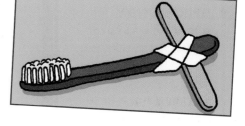

Sharing the game
● Point out in the sky aeroplane contrails (or 'vapour trails').
● Give your child an old soft toothbrush, a lollipop stick and a sticky-tape dispenser.
● Say to your child, 'I wonder what we could turn this toothbrush into'.

● Help your child to turn the toothbrush into whatever she suggests.
● If your child chooses to make an aeroplane, suggest that the lollipop stick be attached with sticky tape at the opposite end to the bristles.
● Put the white paint into the saucer.
● Show your child how to dip the toothbrush into the paint.
● Encourage your child to be a 'pilot' and 'fly' her aeroplane across the paper, looping and swooping, leaving white contrails behind and making appropriate sound effects.

Taking it further
● Make two or three large zigzag squirts of shaving foam on the plain underside of a tray.
● Together, with wet hands, smooth out the foam very lightly over the tray to look like a white sky.
● Ask your child to dry her hands and use her finger(s) to create contrails, patterns or pictures.
● Show your child how to erase these, by very lightly smoothing her wet hands across the foam.
● Invite your child to make a play-dough snail.
● Fasten a length of invisible thread (or silver twine) to it.
● Next, attach the other end of the thread to a table corner with sticky tape.
● Slowly move the snail and watch it leave a trail.

LEARNING OPPORTUNITY
● To feel the shape of objects before drawing them.

YOU WILL NEED
Paper; pencils; different-shaped balloons; fruit and vegetables with distinctive shapes; toy animals and vehicles; dolls in different shapes and sizes.

STEPPING STONE
Use lines to enclose a space, then begin to use these shapes to represent objects.

EARLY LEARNING GOAL
Creative development: Explore colour, texture, shape, form and space in two or three dimensions.

Let's draw!

Sharing the game
● Blow up three different-shaped balloons, for example, round, cylindrical and pear-shaped.
● Talk with your child about whether the shapes of the balloons remind him of other things, for example, a ball, a cucumber, a bell and so on.
● Invite your child to stroke around the shape of each balloon.
● Ask your child to close his eyes, stroke each balloon and identify its shape.

● Hold up each balloon in front of your child and ask him to trace the shape of the outer edge in the air, without touching the balloon.
● Invite your child to draw the outline of each balloon on paper.
● Let your child feel around the edge, or trace in the air, the outlines of fruit and vegetables that have distinctive shapes, such as a banana or chicory, but also toy animals, toy vehicles and dolls in different shapes and sizes, before drawing them.
● As your child feels around the edges, or traces in the air, the shapes of the items, introduce words such as 'straight', 'curved', 'edge', 'corner', 'wide', 'narrow', 'long', 'short' and so on.

Taking it further
● Provide your child with thin wax crayons, pencil crayons or felt-tipped pens and encourage him to practise colouring within the lines of his drawings.
● Invite your child to draw fruit or flowers with white chalk on black paper and colour the picture with coloured chalks.

The value of physical activity for young children cannot be overestimated. Together with exploration through the senses, 'whole body' and manipulative play are the most powerful means of finding out for young children. Physical development in the Foundation Stage involves movement, co-ordination and control, spatial awareness, use of equipment and an awareness of healthy living.

Children use body movements to develop understanding of spatial concepts. See if your child is exploring certain movements in different contexts, and provide further experiences to 'feed in' to these interests.

LIVELY TIMES

MOVEMENT

At the age of three, children delight in moving spontaneously, especially to rhythm, music and stories. By the age of four, they can choose to move in a wide variety of imaginative ways and directions. When children reach five years of age, they can use a combination of movements to express feelings and experiences.

How you can help
● Whenever possible, sing and play with your child. Try to make up spontaneous little songs together about the most routine of your chores and combine them with bold, 'whole body' movements and miming. Your child will love these little 'physical bursts', especially if she has been sitting still for a period of time, and will soon be keen to make up her own little songs.
● Bring your child's favourite stories to life by acting them out together. Make up actions to help her to recall the day, with an accompanying song, for example, 'This is the way Sophia woke up…' to the tune of 'Here We Go Round the Mulberry Bush' (Traditional). Encourage your child to make facial expressions and gestures to convey her feelings. You will find that plastic mirrors are useful for this.

CONTROL AND CO-ORDINATION
Three-year-old children can walk upstairs with one foot on each step, and stand on one foot for a second.

They enjoy the activities involving bending and stretching. By the age of four, children's sense of balance is developing, as is their ability to 'hold' a position. They can now climb stairs and steps, or play on a climbing frame using alternate feet, and begin to hop. At the age of five, children can walk downstairs using alternate feet. Thy are able to jump 'off', 'land' and skip.

How you can help
● Involve your child in as many 'real' jobs as possible, taking safety considerations into account. She will love using a dustpan and brush,

stretching up to give your outfit a 'brush' before you go out, and picking up grass and leaves in the garden.

● Play 'Musical statues' and develop your child's hopping skills by holding both of her hands, initially, before progressing to 'Hopscotch'.

● When your child is approximately four and a half, introduce her to jumping over a skipping rope and other rope skills.

● At five years old, encourage your child to roller-skate.

SPATIAL AWARENESS

Three-year-olds love making up their own routes and journeys such as in shopping play and when they are pushing or pulling buggies, carts and so on. At the age of four, children can take into account the needs of other children playing around them, and by the age of five, most children are showing a clear tendency to be either right- or left-handed.

How you can help

● Follow your child's play interests and allow her as much space as you can to enable her to go 'there and back' from her 'house' to the 'shops' and so on.

● Give your child messages and errands to carry out around the home.

● Encourage her to play group games involving moving around other children without bumping into one another, such as 'Musical bumps', 'Musical chairs' and 'Traffic-lights'.

● If space permits outside, create obstacle courses in the garden for your child to ride around. If, at the age of five, she is showing clear left or right tendencies, teach her the correct terms such as when putting on socks and shoes, laying the table and playing ball and floor 'traffic' games.

● When you are out walking or driving with your child, mention to her when you are turning left or right.

USING SMALL AND LARGE EQUIPMENT

At three and a half, children can usually pedal a tricycle, throw a ball overhand, catch a large ball with extended arms and kick a ball. By four and a half, they are adept at manoeuvring cartons and so on to create dens, are agile on large climbing equipment and can use bats and balls.

How you can help

● Remember to check that your child's tricycle is the correct size and weight. At the age of four, girls tend to need a lighter tricycle than boys do.

● Play with your child 'Throw and catch' games with floaty scarves, crêpe-paper streamers and beanbags.

● Encourage your child to play games with skittles and hoops with other people, and to devise 'home-made' rules.

MANIPULATION

At the age of three, children will persevere with skills needing hand–eye co-ordination such as pairing and cutting. Between the ages of three and a half and four, they develop their drawing and mark-making skills, as well as their dexterity with small objects. By the age of four and a half to five, they are keen to express themselves in pictures, writing and model-making, using techniques and tools safely.

How you can help

● Give your child space and time, and involve her in cooking and carrying cold drinks on a tray, for example.

● Allow your child to carry out plenty of large-scale floor activities such as finger-painting across a length of wallpaper, and counting trains and cars, developing at the same time addition and subtraction skills.

● If your child wants to plan her activities, always chat about her ideas. Assist her only if required and discuss afterwards 'how it went'.

BEING AWARE OF HEALTHY LIVING

At the age of three, children know we must sleep, eat and wash our hands. Four-year-olds have a more detailed awareness of healthy practices, for example, they are beginning to understand how exercise affects the body. By the age of five, they can explain the reasons for a healthy lifestyle.

How you can help

● Encourage independence in self-help skills, an adventurous attitude towards healthy foods from different cultures, and experience of how much fun physical activity can be.

Animal kingdom

LEARNING OPPORTUNITY
● To move like different animals.

YOU WILL NEED
Picture and information books about animals; percussion instruments; tape recorder or CD player; tapes or CDs of animal music such as *Carnival of the Animals* by Saint-Saëns; coloured paper; card; scissors; sticky tape; child's belt.

 STEPPING STONE Move in a range of ways such as slithering, shuffling, rolling, crawling, walking, running, jumping, skipping, sliding and hopping.

 EARLY LEARNING GOAL
Physical development: Move with confidence, imagination and in safety.

Sharing the game

● Look at the animal picture and information books with your child and find out how the animals move.

● Introduce words to your child that describe animal movements, for example, slithering and sliding snakes; shuffling, loping and swinging monkeys; creeping crocodiles; tramping, stamping and swaying elephants, and so on.

● Experiment together with percussion instruments to find sounds to represent animal movements.

● Make simple animal ears for your child to wear. Cut a strip of coloured paper, measure it around your child's head and attach it with sticky tape. Cut out some ears from coloured paper and attach them to the band of paper.

● Create a tail by attaching coloured strips of paper to a child's belt with sticky tape.

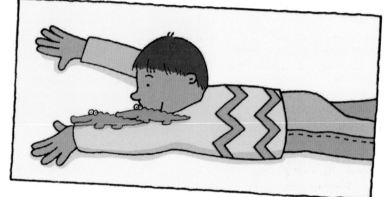

● Play the instruments or animal music and encourage your child to move around like certain animals, making his own sound effects if he wishes.

Taking it further

● Make up simple stories together for your child to act out, based on the factual details in the animal books, and possibly involving the animals' feelings.

● Encourage your child to convey the animals' feelings through both facial expressions and movement, as you say, for example, 'A little elephant was tramping along sadly as she felt lonely. Then, along came another elephant that joined trunks with her to say "hello". They swayed happily to the water hole and sprayed themselves with water'.

● ●

LEARNING OPPORTUNITY
● To appreciate the importance of moving slowly when travelling backwards.

YOU WILL NEED
A baby's or child's plastic safety mirror; string; sticky tape; tin-foil tube; child's sit-and-ride vehicle; two chairs.

THINK FIRST!
When using mirrors with young children, always ensure that they are of the plastic, safety variety.

STEPPING STONE
Go backwards and sideways as well as forwards.

EARLY LEARNING GOAL
Physical development: Move with confidence, imagination and in safety.

I'm reversing

Sharing the game
● When out and about with your child, point out vehicles that are reversing. Talk about why this needs to be done very slowly.
● Show your child interior and exterior mirrors on vehicles and explain what they are used: to look behind when reversing and to know when to stop; to avoid hitting garage doors when reversing into a driveway, and so on.

● At home, encourage your child to stand with her back towards you, a little way away, and to walk backwards, towards you very slowly so that neither of you gets hurt.
● Ask your child to repeat this holding the mirror so that you are in view, and to stop just before she reaches you.
● Attach the tin-foil tube to the sit-and-ride vehicle with string and sticky tape.
● Invite your child to sit in the vehicle, then attach the mirror to the tube with sticky tape at an appropriate height for her to look in it and see what is behind her.
● Stand the chairs a little distance behind your child to represent some garage doors.
● Ask your child to reverse, looking in the mirror at the 'doors', and to stop before hitting them.

Taking it further
● Show your child how to do a three-point turn using her mirror to reverse and to stop before hitting the 'kerb'.

LEARNING OPPORTUNITY
● To use body movement and instruments to create a one-person band.

YOU WILL NEED
Tissue paper; comb; belt; ribbon or string; percussion instruments such as bells, cymbals, tambourines and maracas; tape recorder or CD player; tape or CD of nursery rhymes or songs.

 STEPPING STONE
Combine and repeat a range of movements.

 EARLY LEARNING GOALS
Physical development: Move with control and co-ordination. Travel around, under, over and through balancing and climbing equipment.

Solo bands

Sharing the game
● Talk with your child about circus clowns and street performers who are often one-person bands.
● If possible, take your child to see a circus or street carnival.
● Together, experiment with making different sounds using various body movements, for example, clapping, finger-clicking (if possible), foot-tapping and -stamping, tongue-clucking, humming, singing and so on.
● Try making sounds with the percussion instruments.
● Talk with your child about ideas for 'wearing' as many different instruments as possible at the same time to create a one-person band, for example, bells tied to shoes, cymbals tied around knees, tambourine tied on to the belt at hip level to be played with the elbow, maracas in hands, and tissue paper and comb as mouth organ.
● As you sing a nursery rhyme or song, ask your child to stand still and play it, firstly with one instrument, then two at a time and so on, until he can play all the instruments together.
● When your child is not using the comb and tissue paper, encourage him to sing and accompany himself.
● Ask your child to try playing the instruments while he is walking around accompanied by your singing, his own singing or a music tape or CD.

Taking it further
● Encourage your child to play the instruments quickly, slowly , loudly and quietly.
● Let your child create a puppet band by wearing a glove puppet that can play the percussion instruments.

LEARNING OPPORTUNITY
● To steer a supermarket trolley.

YOU WILL NEED
A vegetable rack on castors or a sit-and-ride vehicle; cardboard box; scissors; string; black felt-tipped pen; small, empty food packets; eight chairs.

 STEPPING STONE
Negotiate an appropriate pathway when walking, running or using a wheelchair or other mobility aids, both indoors and outdoors.

EARLY LEARNING GOAL
Physical development: Show awareness of space, of themselves and of others.

Along the aisles

Sharing the game
● Use the vegetable rack as a trolley.
● Alternatively, draw squares on the sides of the cardboard box with the pen. Make three pairs of holes along two sides of the box using the scissors, then thread string through them and tie the box on to the sit-and-ride vehicle to create a trolley.
● Arrange the chairs to represent a supermarket aisle and place empty food packets on the chairs.
● Ask your child to steer the 'trolley', putting in food packets along the way, up the aisle, turning right or left at the top, and down the next aisle (behind the chair).
● Remind your child to take care not to bump into other shoppers or the shelving.
● Pretend to be another shopper, walking and positioning yourself so that your child will have to steer carefully to avoid you!

Taking it further
● Increase the steering challenge by pushing the chairs closer towards each other to make a narrower aisle.
● Create a supermarket floor on the back of a length of wallpaper.
● Draw aisles and use miniature shop items or stick parts of labels on small bricks.
● Use a small, empty food packet stuck on a set of construction wheels to use as a trolley.
● Create imaginative scenarios with small-world people, animals and so on, involving, for example, a friendly elephant that has escaped from the safari park and visits the supermarket.

LEARNING OPPORTUNITY
● To learn to distinguish between the left and right sides of their bodies.

YOU WILL NEED
A football-sized ball; two cushions.

Left and right goals

Sharing the game
● Put the cushions on the floor in a large area to use as goalposts.
● Invite your child to be the goalkeeper.
● Ask your child to call out 'right' or 'left', depending on which side of his body he would like you to kick the ball.
● Kick the ball towards your child, saying, 'Ball coming to your right!' (or left, as appropriate).

● If your child saves the goal, he wins a point. If not, then you win a point.
● The winner is the first person to collect five points.
● Repeat the game but this time, point to the side that you will kick the ball, instead of telling your child.
● When your child saves a goal, say, 'Well done! You saved that goal on your right-hand side!'.

Taking it further
● Place two cardboard boxes on their sides and mark one 'left' and the other 'right'.
● Invite your child to kick the ball with his left foot into the left box and vice versa.
● Mark two different-coloured skittles 'left' and 'right', then place them next to each other, but not too close together.
● Encourage your child to try to knock down the left-hand skittle by kicking the ball with his left foot and vice versa.
● Invite your child to roll a light football with his right hand and mark out how far it travels using building blocks.
● Give your child the ball again and this time ask him to roll it with his left hand, then mark out how far it travels.
● Ask your child which hand felt the stronger as he rolled the ball.
● Talk with your child about which ball travelled the furthest and ask him why.

STEPPING STONE
Show a clear and consistent preference for the left or right hand.

EARLY LEARNING GOAL
Physical development: Show awareness of space, of themselves and of others.

LEARNING OPPORTUNITY
● To see how physical activity affects their bodies.

YOU WILL NEED
No special requirements.

STEPPING STONE
Observe the effects of activity on their bodies.

EARLY LEARNING GOALS
Physical development: Recognise the importance of keeping healthy and those things which contribute to this. Recognise the changes that happen to their bodies when they are active.

I'm hot!

Sharing the game
● Tell your child that you are going to sing and move to special songs that will help her feel some changes in her body.

● Ask your child to choose an activity such as running, jogging, jumping or hopping.

● Depending on your child's choice, sing and move on the spot, for example:

Verse 1
We are jogging,
jogging, jogging
We are jogging this fine day!

● Encourage your child to say how her body is feeling, for example, heart beating a little faster, feeling a little warmer and so on.

● Continue jogging and singing, for example:
Verse 2
Our hearts are beating faster, faster, faster
Our hearts are beating faster, this fine day!
Verse 3
We are feeling warmer, warmer, warmer
We are feeling warmer, this fine day!

● Substitute jogging for the other actions such as skipping, dancing, swimming, doing press-ups, playing tennis and so on.

Taking it further
● Discuss the consequences of running, twirling and so on for a long time, for example, feeling thirsty and sweaty, or falling over.
● Talk about the remedies for these such as having a drink and a shower, or lying still.

LEARNING OPPORTUNITY
● To pretend to be health and sports instructors.

YOU WILL NEED
Tape recorder or CD player; tapes or CDs of aerobic-type disco music and relaxing music; table; two footballs; cushions; skipping rope; plastic sports sets such as for cricket or golf; comfortable clothing with a few 'specialist' items such as a ballet outfit or football shirt.

STEPPING STONE
Show some understanding that good practices with regard to exercise, eating, sleeping and hygiene can contribute to good health.

EARLY LEARNING GOALS
Physical development:
Recognise the importance of keeping healthy, and those things which contribute to this. Recognise the changes that happen to their bodies when they are active.

Let's get fit!

Sharing the game

● Talk with your child about the importance of exercise to keep healthy and how people go to aerobic classes or take part in a sport.

● Your child will love being an 'instructor' and demonstrating to you exactly what to do in your aerobics class, football training or synchronised-swimming class!

● Encourage your child to verbalise the actions that he wants you to copy, so you can get it exactly right, for example, 'Stretch your arm up right over your head and keep your elbow straight'.

● Ideas for classes, simple props and related vocabulary could include:

Aerobics class – music, warm-up and cool-down sessions

Ballet class – table as 'bar' and 'plié' (legs bent at knee)

Football training – cushions spaced on the floor for 'dribbling' and skipping rope

Synchronised swimming – explain that this is like 'water ballet', then lie on your backs on the floor and devise slow, graceful movements to relaxing music.

Taking it further

● Discuss the importance of eating healthy food and maintaining good hygiene to stay healthy.

● Talk about the need for getting enough sleep in order to grow and maintain our energy levels. Read the rhyme 'Go to Bed' (see page 128).

LEARNING OPPORTUNITY
● To devise large-scale scenes for indoor and outdoor adventure play.

YOU WILL NEED
Teddy bears; soft and plastic animals; cardboard boxes; old curtains; string; cushions; table; chairs. For a 'car wash': sit-and-ride vehicle; two large plastic carrier bags; scissors; string; sticky tape; two plastic-fibre feather dusters.

 THINK FIRST! Never leave young children unsupervised with plastic bags.

 STEPPING STONE Construct with large materials, such as cartons, long lengths of fabric and planks.

⭐ **EARLY LEARNING GOAL** Physical development: Use a range of small and large equipment.

Teddy's car wash

Sharing the game
● Suggest to your child the beginning of an idea for adventure play based on a story.
● Provide a few items such as a cardboard box, cushions and so on.
● Stand back and let your child develop the actions of the adventure as she goes along.
● Join in only if you are invited to. Make brief appearances in role, for example, as the pirate ship's cook, with some 'barnacle' cookies, just enough to help the play along, if necessary.
● Ideas could include:

A journey – in a 'pirate ship' cardboard box to a 'treasure island' where teddies may sleep in a curtain 'hammock' between two chairs;

An experience – at a 'car wash'. Cut open a carrier bag down one side and along the bottom and make slits; cut open the other carrier bag down both sides, open it out and tie it across two chairs with string to create a 'roof'; attach string to the front of the vehicle to pull

it along as it comes through the 'car wash' (between the chairs).

Attach the first bag at a right angle with sticky tape. As teddy's car comes through the 'car wash', both of you should twirl a feather duster each.

Taking it further
● Ask your child to dictate her adventure for you to write as a story.
● Let your child illustrate the story.

Busy ball

Sharing the game

● Together, roll up some toilet tissue into a loose ball, approximately 30cm in circumference.

● Secure the end with sticky tape.

● Cut off one leg from the pair of tights.

● Cut off the foot and knot the end.

● Carefully push the ball of toilet tissue down to the knotted end.

● Make another knot just above the ball.

● Help your child to practise some ball skills, for example:

● throwing upwards and catching

● throwing to you and catching (start at 25cm apart from each other and throw very gently)

● rolling to each other

● kicking to each other and into an open box turned on to its side

● swinging – swing the ball from side to side, backwards and forwards and, outside, round and round in the air, like a wheel and above your head.

Taking it further

● Encourage your child to help you to make another 'busy ball' using the whole length of the leg of tights.

● Tie the ball to a branch of a tree or a washing line that has lots of space around.

● Give your child a small bat to hit the ball.

YOU WILL NEED
A piece of card from a cardboard box, approximately 30cm x 30cm; ten pieces of wool, approximately 40cm long; sticky tape; scissors; clear nail varnish; non-poisonous leaves, grasses, flowers and so on.

THINK FIRST!
Always keep substances that can be inhaled, such as nail varnish, away from children.

STEPPING STONE
Engage in activities requiring hand–eye co-ordination.

EARLY LEARNING GOAL
Physical development: Handle tools, objects, construction and malleable materials safely and with increasing control.

Leaf weaving

Sharing the game
● Before the activity, and away from your child, dip the ends of the pieces of wool into clear nail varnish to make them easier to thread.
● Using the points of the scissors, pierce holes around the edge of the piece of cardboard, approximately 5cm apart.

● Pierce from both sides of the card to achieve clean holes.
● Thread the end of one piece of wool through the hole in the top left-hand corner of the card if your child is right-handed, or through the hole in the top right-hand side if she is left-handed, and secure it with sticky tape.
● Help your child to thread the wool in vertical lines, securing the end of each piece of wool with sticky tape on the back of the card.
● Turn the card on its 'side' and ask your child to repeat the threading process to make squares.
● Encourage your child to thread leaves, grasses and flowers through the squares.

Taking it further
● Invite your child to make a bookmark by cutting a rectangle, approximately 15cm x 4cm, from an old greetings card.
● Ask your child to make holes around the edge of the rectangle with a hole-punch.
● Let her thread wool through the holes, leaving two ends at the bottom to be knotted as a 'tassel'.

LEARNING OPPORTUNITY
● To explore the properties of tin foil.

YOU WILL NEED
Tin foil; old keys; coins; scissors; buttons; jewellery; potato masher; shells; ridged leaves; old greetings cards; pen; sticky tape.

STEPPING STONE
Explore malleable materials by patting, stroking, poking, squeezing, pinching and twisting them.

EARLY LEARNING GOAL
Physical development: Handle tools, objects, construction and malleable materials safely and with increasing control.

Silversmith

Sharing the game
● Your child will find it very satisfying to fold, press, smooth, roll, bend and squeeze tin foil.
● Give your child simple things to wrap in foil such as a dessertspoon, banana, bar of soap and so on.
● Let your child make 'pressings' by putting foil on top of items such as keys, coins, scissors, buttons, jewellery, shells, a potato masher and ridged leaves. Encourage him to press and rub with his fingertips or the side of his hand.
● Let your child make 'foil coil' sculptures. Cut out a strip of foil, approximately 20cm x 8cm. Help him to fold it in half lengthways three times, to make a narrow band.

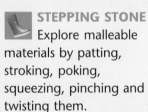

● Ask your child to wrap the band tightly around a pen, and then to gently slide it off to make a coil.
● Make three or four coils.
● Cover a greetings card in foil and attach the coils to make a '3-D abstract sculpture'.

Taking it further
● Make a 'scented basket' by covering a small, shallow plastic mousse or margarine pot with foil.
● Help your child to make a 'handle' from a foil strip, gently rolled and squeezed and attached to the pot with sticky tape.
● Cut around the inner circle of a doily and gently secure some of the outer doily edge around the sides of the 'basket' with sticky tape.
● Invite your child to spoon some pot pourri into the 'basket'.

Chocolate boxes

Sharing the game
● Invite your child to look at the different kinds of modelling materials and to explore their different properties.

● Encourage your child to look at the different chocolate shapes and the designs on them and to match them on the 'choice' card.

● Talk about the names of the shapes and introduce words to

describe the designs, for example, lines, squiggles, swirls, zigzags and ridges.

● Ask your child to make some 'chocolates' using the modelling material. (If you use colours other than brown, call the chocolates 'Rainbow chocolates'.)

● Give your child some tools, for example, a comb, fork, pen and ridged felt-tipped-pen top, to experiment with making designs.

● Let your child fill the empty chocolate box with her 'replica' chocolates.

Taking it further
● Ask your child to look at the skins of fruit and vegetables such as pineapple, strawberry, orange and celery through a plastic magnifying glass.

● Invite your child to make some model miniature fruit and vegetables.

● Let her put her 'fruit' in a 'fruit bowl', for example, a small, transparent cherry-tomato container, and her 'vegetables' in a 'harvest hamper', for example a miniature basket.

● Encourage your child to use modelling materials to make attractive 2-D and 3-D pictures.

WINDING DOWN

Children learn a great deal incidentally and informally, especially through relaxed chatting. This chapter begins with some fun bathtime games that can, of course, be played at any time such as in a washing-up bowl, at a sink, at a water tray in a setting, or in a garden paddling pool. Although the games in this chapter focus on developing children's knowledge and understanding of the world, they will also, at the same time, help to develop their language skills by adding to children's vocabulary, as well as give them practice in using words to help develop their thinking skills.

LISTENING
From being babies, all children love nursery rhymes and songs, especially when combined with physical movement, as in action songs and rhymes. Three-year-olds join in these games enthusiastically, and love to match their movements to the words, such as in 'The hokey cokey'. They enjoy recognising different environmental sounds, animal noises and people's voices. By the age of four, children can identify which words rhyme with one another, and are starting to develop an awareness of alliteration by recognising whether pairs of words begin with the same sound or not. Five-year-olds love to make up 'nonsense rhyming strings' involving their names, for example, 'Charlie, Barlie, Farlie,

Marlie'. This is excellent practice for learning to hear the different sounds at the beginnings of words.

How you can help
● As with your child's physical development, make the singing of nursery rhymes and songs a regular and spontaneous part of your daily lives, often leaving pauses for him to complete the rhyme.
● Cover a table or two chairs with a sheet and take turns to sit behind it and play 'Guess the sound' games, for example, pouring water into a bowl.
● Record the voices of relatives and friends on to a tape for your child to identify.
● To develop an awareness of alliteration, make an 'alphabet book' of the first names of people that your child knows, preceded by another word beginning with the same sound, for example, 'Baking Ben', 'Swimming Sally' and so on.

● Play lots of 'mini games' of 'I spy', for example, 'I spy something beginning/ ending with "p"'. Specify where you are looking, such as 'something on the curtain pattern', or 'something in the vegetable rack'.

SPEAKING

Three-year-olds tell long 'stories' to themselves, in the present tense, as they play, for example, with small-world toys. As they love hearing their favourite stories many times, they can begin to retell them in part. At the age of four, they can use the past tense and begin to use words to 'represent' items not physically present, as well as thoughts and experiences. They also enjoy making up their own stories. By the age of five, children can predict and explain situations, and they love jokes.

How you can help

● Join in your child's activities, but be led by him.

● Use a 'running commentary' sensitively, without turning it into a monologue!

● When your child makes a mistake in speaking, gently repeat what he said, using the correct word, tense and so on.

● Read as many stories as possible to your child to develop his vocabulary and sequential thinking skills, for example, 'And what happened then?'.

● Talk about characters' feelings, motivations, notions of 'fair play' and alternative endings.

● Develop your child's skills at making up stories by using glove puppets 'in narrative conversation', for example, 'So what did you do then?'.

● Play 'ping-pong' stories with your child, each thinking up the next event in a story. Use small-world items as prompts to start the stories with.

Children need words to think, as they develop from being primarily concerned with the 'here and now', using mainly the present tense in their language. Gradually, children become able to think in the abstract. They begin to use words as symbols to represent objects not literally 'there', as well as memories, thoughts, feelings, wishes, ideas and plans for the future. At this stage, children need, and begin to use, the past and present tense in order to express themselves, for example, 'I expect Teddy did that because he was feeling angry. I hope he'll say sorry'. The rest of the chapter focuses on activities to develop children's listening, speaking and thinking skills – their ability to hear and say rhymes, play 'I spy', retell familiar stories and make up their own, and start to use language as a tool for thinking.

It's raining

Sharing the game

● Ask your child to create a street scene on the bottom of the large plastic bowl using small-world people, cars and buildings.
● Say, 'Oh, dear! It's starting to spit with rain!' and demonstrate to your child how to use the eye-dropper to simulate rain 'spitting' on the street.

● Then say, 'Oh, it's starting to drizzle, now' and show your child how to use the plant sprayer to create a fine 'drizzle' of rain.
● Say, 'It's raining properly, now' and give your child the watering can.
● Continue with 'pouring down', using the jug, then 'bucketing down', using the bucket.
● Refill the containers and repeat the process in reverse, starting with 'bucketing down', saying each time, 'Good! The rain is slowing down a little'.

Taking it further

● Invite your child to hold her hand out above the bowl.
● Using each container in turn, let the water fall gently on the back of your child's hand so that she can see and feel the difference between each 'rain level'. Remember to dry her hand each time.
● Ask your child to close her eyes and see if she can identify the different 'levels' of water.
● Close your eyes and ask your child to pour the different 'rain levels' on your hand, identifying each one as she does so, for example, 'It's drizzling now!'.

●●●●●●●●●●●●●●●●●●●●●●●●●●●●●●●

LEARNING OPPORTUNITY
● To differentiate between different degrees of rainfall.

YOU WILL NEED
Water; large plastic bowl; water tray or bath (at bathtime); small-world people, cars and buildings; containers filled with water, such as an eye-dropper, plant sprayer, child's watering can, jug and beach bucket.

 THINK FIRST! Never leave children unsupervised when playing with water.

STEPPING STONE Describe simple features of objects and events.

EARLY LEARNING GOAL
Knowledge and understanding of the world: Investigate objects and materials by using all of their senses as appropriate.

YOU WILL NEED
A copy of *The Three Billy Goats Gruff* (First Favourite Tales series, Ladybird Books); large plastic bowl or bath filled with water; construction sets such as Duplo or Sticklebricks; set of animals to represent the Three Billy Goats Gruff (large, medium and small); modelling material such as play dough or Plasticine; pen.

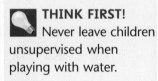

THINK FIRST!
Never leave children unsupervised when playing with water.

STEPPING STONE
Talk about what is seen and what is happening.

EARLY LEARNING GOAL
Knowledge and understanding of the world: Look closely at similarities, differences, patterns and change.

Story bridges

Sharing the game
● Tell your child the story of the Three Billy Goats Gruff.
● Ask your child to construct a bridge with his construction toys to place in the bowl.
● Assemble the goats. If the animals that you are using are different from goats, explain to your child that it is fun to adapt a story and change it.
● Invite your child to make a troll from the modelling material, using a pen point for its features.
● Act out the story together.
● Notice with your child the amount of 'splash' when the troll is tossed into the water.
● Lower the bridge and point out how much less 'splash' there is.
● Raise the bridge as high as possible and ask your child to predict how much 'splash' there will be, and to try to say why.

Taking it further
● Talk about the game of 'Pooh sticks' from *The House at Pooh Corner* by AA Milne (Methuen Children's Books) in which Winnie-the-Pooh and his friends toss sticks into a river from a bridge, run to the other side and see whose stick appears first.
● If possible, play 'Pooh sticks' from a real bridge and explain to your child that water in a real river flows towards the sea.

WINDING DOWN

LEARNING OPPORTUNITY
● To investigate the properties of sponges and facecloths.

YOU WILL NEED
Several kinds of sponges (two of which are identical and two of which are of equal size), for example, washing-up, bath and shower; scissors; two transparent plastic cups; facecloth.

THINK FIRST!
Never leave children unsupervised when playing with water.

STEPPING STONE
Show an awareness of change.

EARLY LEARNING GOAL
Knowledge and understanding of the world: Look closely at similarities, differences, patterns and change.

Squeezy, squeezy!

Sharing the game
● Provide your child with two identical sponges.
● Ask your child to describe how they feel, for example, 'dry', 'light', 'springy' and so on.
● Encourage your child to submerge the sponges in water and to describe them again, for example, 'wet', 'heavy', 'soggy' and so on.
● Invite your child to squeeze them tightly into the cups.
● Talk about the water that the sponges have absorbed.
● On another occasion, give your child two sponges of equal size, but different textures, for example, a light

bath sponge and a denser shower sponge to compare how much water each one can absorb. Explain that, although one sponge might be larger, it could absorb less water because it is made from a different kind of material that holds less water.
● Encourage your child to predict, then compare, the amounts of water absorbed by a sponge and a facecloth.

Taking it further
● Talk about and, if possible, show your child the gel-filled pad inside a disposable nappy, which absorbs the moisture from a baby to keep the baby dry.
● Discuss and, if possible, show your child a towelling nappy and point out that nappies, facecloths and towels are all made from the same material.
● Explain to your child that disposable nappies, towelling nappies and sponges are all absorbent, but point out that babies' nappies are never made from sponges.

LEARNING OPPORTUNITY
● To realise the weight of water.

YOU WILL NEED
Two or three different-sized polythene sandwich bags; tie tags; six plastic cups; water.

THINK FIRST! Never leave children unsupervised when playing with water or using polythene bags.

STEPPING STONE Show curiosity, observe and manipulate objects.

EARLY LEARNING GOAL
Knowledge and understanding of the world: Investigate objects and materials by using all of their senses as appropriate.

Squelchy, squelchy!

Sharing the game
● Show your child the three different-sized bags and talk about which one is the 'small' bag, the 'medium-sized' bag and the 'large' bag.
● Ask your child to say which bag would hold the 'most' water, which the 'least' water, and which the 'medium' amount of water.
● Put the bags side by side in a row and ask your child which bag would hold three cupfuls of water, which one

would hold two cupfuls and which one would only hold one cupful.
● Together, fill the bags with three, two and one cupful(s) of water, respectively, securing each bag with a tie tag.
● Encourage your child to predict which bag would feel the 'heaviest', which the 'lightest' and which one would feel 'in between' or 'of medium weight'.
● Let your child feel the weight of the bags to see if he was correct.
● Ask your child to close his eyes and try to tell which bag is which, when you put them in his hands.

Taking it further
● Pierce three holes in the large bag, two in the medium bag and one in the small bag.
● Let your child have fun squeezing out the water.

LEARNING OPPORTUNITY
● To explore the use of funnels.

YOU WILL NEED
A plastic funnel; empty 5-litre plastic container such as one used for washing-up liquid; empty washing-up-liquid bottle; empty large shampoo bottle.

💡 **THINK FIRST!** Never leave children unsupervised when playing with water.

🔨 **STEPPING STONE** Show an interest in why things happen and how things work.

⭐ **EARLY LEARNING GOAL**
Knowledge and understanding of the world: Look closely at similarities and differences, patterns and change.

Fun with funnels

Sharing the game
● Show your child the plastic funnel and ask her what she thinks it is used for.
● Tell your child that funnels are useful when we have to pour a liquid from a wide-mouthed container into a narrow-mouthed container without spilling it.
● Say that some people like to buy washing-up liquid in large containers, but they are too big and too heavy to use at the kitchen sink, so the liquid needs to be poured into a smaller, empty washing-up liquid bottle.
● Show your child the wide opening of the 5-litre container and the narrow opening of the washing-up bottle and explain that it is difficult to pour the liquid into the bottle without spilling it.
● Show your child how the top of the funnel is wide and how the bottom is narrow.
● Put some water into the container and encourage your child to funnel it into the bottle.
● Tell your child that hairdressers can buy some of their shampoo in

large containers, which they then 'funnel' into smaller bottles. Give your child the shampoo bottle and see if she can fill it using the funnel.

Taking it further
● Let your child make a 'musical funnel' by putting the end of the funnel inside a short length of rubber or plastic tubing (available from hardware shops).
● Ask your child to hum or sing through the tube.

Pillow rhymes

Sharing the game

● Read some nursery rhymes to your child and pause before the second rhyming word for your child to complete, for example, 'Jack and Jill went up the…'.

● Draw a simple picture on a piece of paper of something that obviously does not rhyme, for example, a tree instead of a hill.

● Ask your child to close his eyes while you put the picture under his pillow.

● Let your child open his eyes, then start saying the nursery rhyme again together, pausing before the second rhyming word.

● Encourage your child to look under his pillow and find the picture.

● Ask your child, 'Does that picture rhyme?'.

● Recite the rhyme with the 'wrong' word to hear how it sounds.

● Occasionally, draw something that does rhyme, such as bricks, but is not the correct word in the rhyme, for example, 'Five, six, pick up bricks', instead of 'sticks'.

● Vary the wording to generate new rhymes, for example, 'Jill and Jack went up the track…'.

Taking it further

● Play 'nonsense rhyming strings'. Show your child an object with a one-syllable name, for example, a pen.

● Slowly repeat a different initial sound six times, then pause, for example, 's, s, s, s, s, s'.

● Ask your child to say the 'new' word by substituting the 's' sound for the 'p' sound, for example, 'sen'.

LEARNING OPPORTUNITY
● To hear and say initial sounds, and link some letters with their sounds.

YOU WILL NEED
A torch; alphabet frieze; alphabet poster or alphabet books; picture book; 26 magnetic alphabet letters on metal board.

STEPPING STONE
Hear and say the initial sound in words and know which letters represent some of the sounds.

EARLY LEARNING GOAL
Communication, language and literacy: Hear and say initial and final sounds in words, and short vowel sounds within words.

Bedtime 'I spy'

Sharing the game
● Turn off the light and shine the torch on two adjacent pictures on your child's alphabet frieze, poster or in an alphabet book.
● Say, 'I spy with my little eye something beginning with (for example) "s". Is it a "snake" or "television"?'. Give your child the choice of the two words.
● When your child is able to answer this, say, 'One, two, three, please tell me what sound "snake" begins with'. If she tells you the correct sound, place the board of magnetic letters on your knee and put the relevant two adjacent letters in her hand, for example, 's' and 't'.
● Then say, 'One, two, three, please show me which letter "snake" begins with'.
● Ask your child to show and give you the initial letter of 'snake'.
● When your child is comfortable with playing 'I spy', saying the initial sound herself and giving you the matching initial letter, shine the torch on three adjacent pictures at a time and play the same game.

● When your child can do this confidently, increase the 'choice' by shining the torch on a section of a picture in a book and choosing a word on which to focus the game.

Taking it further
● Play the same game, using the final sound of a word, for example, 'I spy with my little eye, something ending with…'.

LEARNING OPPORTUNITY
● To tell a well-known story to a toy.

YOU WILL NEED
A well-loved toy, for example, a teddy bear or cuddly toy; miniature bed, for example, doll's cot, cradle or cardboard box; bedclothes; miniature cuddly toy such as a bear or rabbit; chair; story-books.

 STEPPING STONE Describe main story settings, events and principal characters.

 EARLY LEARNING GOAL Communication, language and literacy: Enjoy listening to and using spoken and written language, and readily turn to it in their play and learning.

Toys' story time

Sharing the game
● Just before telling your child his bedtime story, ask if he would like to tell a story to one of his toys.
● Invite your child to choose a cuddly toy, then, together, find or make a 'bed' for it. Put the toy in the bed and place the bed on a

chair next to your child's bed. However, if your child prefers, simply put the toy in his bed next to him.
● Find a miniature cuddly toy for your child's toy to hold.
● Say to your child, 'Which story do you think Teddy (or whatever the name of the cuddly toy is) would like to hear tonight?'.
● Encourage your child to help you to choose a book, ideally one that he is familiar with and that has lots of large pictures that he can talk about.
● Prop the book open between your child and his toy, and help him to 'read' the story.
● Add a word or two, from time to time, to help your child to maintain the pace, turning the pages when necessary and adding phrases at the correct moment, for example, 'and then', 'and in the end' and so on.

Taking it further
● Together, 'ask' the toy to 'say what he thinks is going to happen next' in the story, for example, on the next page.
● Help your child to think up an alternative story ending.

LEARNING OPPORTUNITY
● To make up their own stories.

YOU WILL NEED
A photocopy of a photograph of your child; small-world person; scissors; sticky tape; large tray; toy vehicles such as car, train, boat, aeroplane and rocket; small-world people and animals; toy food; pencil drawings or toys to represent 'locations' and the weather, such as buildings, mountains, flowers, playground, beach, sea, jungle, forest, farm and the moon.

 STEPPING STONE
Begin to use talk to pretend imaginary situations.

EARLY LEARNING GOAL
Communication, Language and Literacy: Use language to imagine and re-create roles and experiences.

My dream story

Sharing the game
● Cut out your child's face from the photocopy and stick it on to a small-world person with sticky tape so that it looks like your child!
● Place the 'small-world child', together with the other toys, on the tray and put them on her bed at bedtime.
● Ask your child to think of a lovely story about herself that she would like to dream about.
● Give your child the 'small-world child' to hold and gently prompt her by showing her the toys in sequence, for example, travelling in a magic vehicle on a long journey, meeting interesting people and animals on the way, eating delicious food, arriving at an amazing destination in the rain, sun and snow, having an adventure there, returning home and being back in bed by the morning.

Taking it further
● The next morning, ask your child if her dream came true, and whether she dreamed about her story. Say that sometimes we have lovely dreams, but we cannot always remember them.
● Invite your child to draw a picture of herself in bed on one side of a sheet of A4 paper, then help her to write her dream story on the back.

You never know!

Sharing the game

● If you and your child are going to do something on a particular day, read a bedtime story the night before relating to the activity.

● As you read the story, casually mention that sometimes similar events happen in 'real life'.

● If possible, talk about something that happened in your childhood that reminds you of a story.

● The next day, devise a scenario that echoes the previous night's story, but do not draw your child's attention to it. See if he can make the link himself and go on to speculate about what might happen next!

● Some ideas could include:

The Three Bears

The next morning, when you are making breakfast, say that something is 'too hot', such as the cereal or toast. Suggest that you go into another room to do something else until it 'cools down'. Unknown to your child, you have hidden one of his toy animals, such

as a tiger, in his bed. While your child is occupied, quickly make it apparent that his breakfast has been eaten! Then discover the sleeping tiger together. As the tiger has not broken any chairs, you decide that he is well behaved and just hungry, so he can stay and live with you!

Jack and the Beanstalk
Plant some seeds the next day, and say, 'Perhaps they are magic…'.

Taking it further

● Create a zigzag book and let your child draw some pictures about his story.

LEARNING OPPORTUNITY
● To describe objects of interest to them.

YOU WILL NEED
A shopping catalogue; scissors; two toy (or disused) telephones; approximately half a metre of crêpe bandage.

STEPPING STONE
Use vocabulary focused on objects and people who are of particular importance to them.

EARLY LEARNING GOAL
Communication, language and literacy: Extend their vocabulary, exploring the meanings and sounds of new words.

By telephone

Sharing the game
● Cut a page of items from the catalogue that are of interest to your child, for example, bicycles, toys, jewellery, clothes and so on.
● Give your child the page from the catalogue, and both of you a telephone, then sit back to back on the floor.
● Loosely wrap the bandage around one of your ankles.
● Pretend that you have hurt your ankle and cannot go shopping, but you need to buy a birthday present for… (a relative or friend).
● Tell your child that you have decided to telephone a shop to ask the 'shopkeeper' (your child) about what she has 'in stock'.

● Telephone the 'shopkeeper' and ask, 'Do you have any rings in stock at the moment, please? Can you tell me what they look like?'.
● Prompt your child to describe, for example, one or two rings on the page, ask about the number and colour of stones, the shape and whether the band is silver or gold.
● Ask your child guided questions such as, 'Is it a ruby or an emerald stone in the middle?'.
● Enquire about the price of the ring, then say, 'Thank you very much for the information. I will come to your shop to see the rings as soon as my ankle is better. Goodbye!'.
● Wrap the bandage around your child's leg and reverse the roles.

Taking it further
● Let your child be a doctor, vet, car mechanic or plumber, who, in answer to your questions, describes an 'operation' or 'repair'.

And because of that...

Sharing the game

● Look at a picture book with your child and make comments such as, 'Hmmm! I think he might have to… What do you think?'.

● Ask questions to help your child to begin to think and talk in the abstract, such as using past and future tenses instead of just the present tense, for example:

Past – 'Why did something happen? Because…'.

Future – 'What might happen next? Perhaps…'.

● Ask questions starting with 'Why…?', 'What could (or should)…?', 'What if…?' and so on, for example, 'Why did the troll not want the goats to go over his bridge?', 'What could (or should) Little Red Riding Hood have done when the wolf spoke to her?' and so on.

● Encourage your child to use phrases such as 'I suppose', 'I expect' and 'Maybe'.

● Play 'And because of that…'. Make a factual statement to your child, for example, 'I went to bed late last night'.

● Ask your child to say, 'And because of that…'.

● Supply some simple 'consequences', for example, 'I woke up late and was late for work'.

● Repeat several times, then reverse the roles.

● When your child is confident, make the 'consequences' more elaborate, for example, 'I woke up late, had no breakfast, broke the heel on my shoe running from the car park to the office, was late for work and was hungry until lunch time!'.

Taking it further

● Make up longer stories together.

FAVOURITE RHYMES

The rhymes on the following pages provide opportunities to introduce lots of new skills while having plenty of fun! They cover growing up, looking at numbers, the world around us, and fun and games.

Letters

Every morning at eight o'clock
You can hear the postman's knock.
Up jumps Katy to open the door,
One letter, two letters, three letters,
 FOUR.

Anonymous

USING THE RHYME
Substitute your child's name for 'Katy' and put four 'pretend' letters on the floor, addressed to your child, with a used stamp stuck on to each letter.

Alternatively, substitute the following for the last line of the rhyme – 'She/He sees a special letter lying on the floor'. Ask a relative, such as a grandparent, to send a real letter inviting your child for a visit, with a tear-off slip for your child to fill in and send back to 'Grandma' or 'Grandad'.

I Can

I can tie my shoelace
I can comb my hair
I can wash my hands and face
And dry myself with care

I can brush my teeth, too
And button up my frocks
I can say 'How do you do?'
And put on both my socks.

Anonymous

USING THE RHYME
Put a shoelace, comb, flannel, small towel, toothbrush, button and pair of socks on to a tray. As you say the rhyme together, ask your child to hold the appropriate item and mime its use. (Also see page 10.)

Five Fat Sausages

Five fat sausages, sizzling in a pan
Sizzle, sizzle, sizzle!
One went 'BANG'!

Four fat sausages…

Adapted from 'Ten Fat Sausages' (Traditional)

USING THE RHYME

For a teatime treat, roll up a nutritious filling in five tortilla-wrap 'sausages' and warm them through in a microwave or conventional oven. For decorative purposes only, present in a cold frying pan on the table! (Also see page 46.)

One Elephant

One elephant went out to play
On a spider's web one day.
He had such enormous fun,
He asked another elephant to come.

Two elephants came out to play…

Anonymous

USING THE RHYME

Together, make a spider's web design, on a large plain plate, with black writing icing. Draw small elephants on pieces of card, then say the rhyme, putting the elephants on the web. Talk about 'one more' each time. (Also see page 45.)

FAVOURITE RHYMES

Chimney Pot

I'm going to build a chimney pot,
I'll build it very high,
I'll build it with my bricks,
And I'll make it touch the sky –
One, two, three, four, five,
Six, seven, eight, nine, ten.
Here comes the wind and here comes the rain,
To knock my chimney down again.

Anonymous

USING THE RHYME
Make the 'demolition vehicle' on page 63. Substitute the penultimate line of the rhyme with 'Here comes the ball and here comes the chain'.

I Hear Thunder

I hear thunder, I hear thunder
(stamp feet on floor)
Hark, don't you, hark, don't you?
(put hand to ear)
Pitter-patter raindrops,
*(move hand down slowly,
waggling fingers)*
Pitter-patter raindrops,
I'm wet through –
(shake body)
You are too!
(point to someone else)

Traditional

USING THE RHYME
Create a 'rainmaker' for the 'pitter-patter' sound by putting grains of rice inside a kitchen-roll tube sealed at both ends with paper and sticky tape. Rotate it slowly. (Also see page 72.)

FAVOURITE RHYMES

Star Light

Star light, star bright,
First star I see tonight,
I wish I may, I wish I might,
Have the wish I wish tonight.

Anonymous

Go to Bed

Go to bed early – wake up with joy
Go to bed late – cross girl or boy
Go to bed early – ready for play
Go to bed late – tired all day.

Go to bed early – no pains or ills
Go to bed late – doctor and pills.
Go to bed early – grow very tall
Go to bed late – stay very small.

Anonymous